Unlock psychology

in 10 concise chapters

Unlock

psychology

in 10 concise chapters

Emily Ralls & Tom Collins

SIRIUS

This edition published in 2025 by Sirius Publishing, a division of
Arcturus Publishing Limited,
26/27 Bickels Yard, 151–153 Bermondsey Street,
London SE1 3HA

Copyright © Arcturus Holdings Limited

All rights reserved. No part of this publication may be reproduced, stored in a retrieval system, or transmitted, in any form or by any means, electronic, mechanical, photocopying, recording or otherwise, without prior written permission in accordance with the provisions of the Copyright Act 1956 (as amended). Any person or persons who do any unauthorised act in relation to this publication may be liable to criminal prosecution and civil claims for damages.

ISBN: 978-1-3988-5171-9
AD011637UK

Printed in China

CONTENTS

Introduction
WHAT IS PSYCHOLOGY? 6

Chapter 1
STRUCTURALIST THEORY 10

Chapter 2
PSYCHODYNAMIC THEORY 22

Chapter 3
GESTALT THEORY 34

Chapter 4
BEHAVIOURISM 50

Chapter 5
COGNITIVE PSYCHOLOGY 62

Chapter 6
HUMANISTIC APPROACH 74

Chapter 7
POSITIVE PSYCHOLOGY 84

Chapter 8
BIOLOGICAL THEORY 94

Chapter 9
SOCIAL PSYCHOLOGY 104

Chapter 10
DEBATES IN PSYCHOLOGY 116

Index 126

Picture Credits 128

WHAT IS PSYCHOLOGY?

IT IS IMPOSSIBLE TO SAY when people first began to think about thinking and to some extent we all act as psychologists. We are continuously making judgements based on our knowledge and understanding of the world. We think about our own actions and reflect on how we might change our decisions in the future. We also observe others around us, looking for intention and deciding how best to react in a given situation. Psychology as we understand it today is the systematic study of how we think, what influences our behaviour and ultimately who we are.

How we approach the study of the human mind has varied hugely over time and between different schools of thought. Some methods can be subjective while others take an objective approach seeking to quantify the human experience. Some methods may also be holistic and may generalize, while others can be reductionist or deterministic, focusing on individual traits. These approaches have been influenced by the politics and thinking of their time as well as the technologies available to the researchers, many of whom sought unique and original solutions. Like the classical sciences, a series of tools developed to study the mind in a scientific way. Modern psychology attempts a more mechanistic approach, taking the view that our mental processes are a by-product of our physical body.

Perhaps the most important tool in the study of psychology is the human mind itself. The brain is extraordinarily large when compared to other animals. While only accounting for 2–3 per cent of our body weight our brain consumes 25 per cent of our energy. We are not sure exactly what drove

WHAT IS PSYCHOLOGY? >>

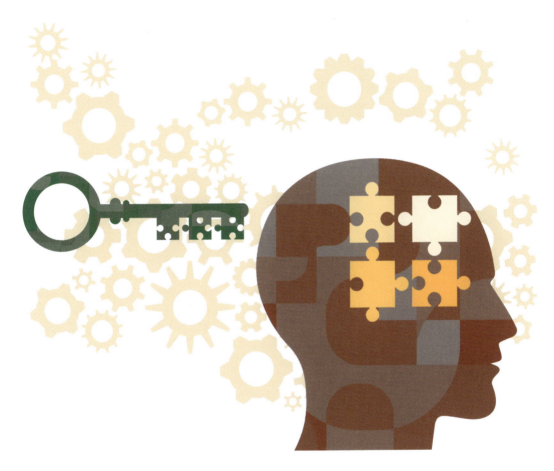

the evolution of our brain size but it led to a cognitive revolution in humans where we began thinking more deeply about the world around us. However, cerebral power is not just a function of size. The structure of the brain is also an important component of cognitive function and who we are as a species.

Humans also evolved in social groups. This meant we developed behaviours and mechanisms for cooperating in groups, as well as complex emotions in order to establish social hierarchy. Being able to communicate, empathize and build trust with other members of the family unit was important to early humans some 70,000 years ago. It has also left a legacy of anxieties and mental disorders that we, as modern humans, can suffer from,

Psychology seeks to unlock the mysteries of the brain.

<< INTRODUCTION

such as being ostracized from a group leading to feelings of sadness and depression. We have also inherited a vast capacity to think and theorize about the world around us and it is in this regard that we are perhaps a unique species.

Psychology as we know it is a relatively modern science with most progress occurring over the last 150 years. Prior to the 19th century, psychology took many forms and ideologies and was often referred to as 'mental philosophy'. The origins of philosophical thinking about the nature of consciousness and the human mind can be traced as far back as ancient Greece in the 5th century BC. Aristotle (384–322 BC) theorized about the mind, considering the soul and physical body to be separate entities. This was established as dualism in the 17th century by the French philosopher René Descartes when he hypothesized that the mind and body connected through the base of the brain via a small structure called the pineal gland.

The study of psychology can be traced as far back as Aristotle.

The belief in dualism persisted until the English philosophers Thomas Hobbes and John Locke conceived of a unified approach between human consciousness and the material world. This alternative approach became known as 'monism' and argued that our mental processes resulted from physical processes taking place in the brain, rather than operating separately.

Despite the development of these approaches and ways of thinking about human consciousness, they are not what we would recognize as modern psychology. By the 18th century, philosophy and psychology had reached a critical juncture. Immanuel Kant had done much to advance on earlier schools of thought. He saw that our mental experience was connected to the physical world and that we could make causal relationships and judgements based on our experiences and knowledge of the world around us. He went as far as developing the idea that a unity of mind or sense of self develops from these experiences. Today we might describe this as an ego. However, Kant was a resolute critic of empirical psychology and insisted that objective study of the soul was a futile enterprise. He argued that it would be impossible to measure one's inner mental processes objectively and saw psychology as being distinctly different from the natural and exact sciences that could be measured and quantified in the material world.

This view brought Kant into conflict with the early psychologists but his criticism also inspired psychologists to take the next leap. Wilhelm Wundt took this next step in the 19th century, seeking to investigate the mind in a systematic and objective way which eventually became known as 'introspection'. It is here that we begin our journey through the different schools of thought in psychology. Over the following ten chapters we discuss these along with some of the core protagonists that helped to establish psychology as a science in its own right.

Immanuel Kant.

Chapter 1
STRUCTURALIST THEORY

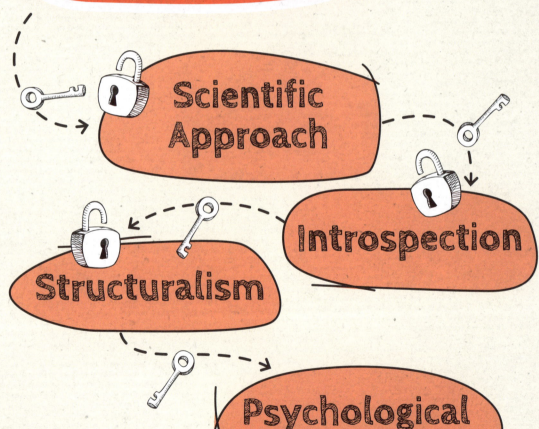

STRUCTURALIST THEORY

STRUCTURALISM IS CONSIDERED a foundational approach in psychology. It was centred on the process of introspection, the procedure of examining your own thoughts, feelings and actions. Using these methods researchers hoped to gain an insight into the inner workings of the mind.

Structuralism is associated with the work of Wilhelm Wundt (1832–1920) and his student Edward Titchener (1867–1927). Considered to be one of the founding fathers of psychology, Wundt led the first attempts to understand the mind in an objective, scientific way. Although the methods used for introspection were individual and subjective the approach was a step forward in establishing psychology as an observable science rather than a philosophical undertaking. Therefore, the structuralist approach is important as it is one of the first attempts to understand the human mind and the elements that make up human consciousness.

ASSUMPTIONS

Structuralism aimed to understand the structure of the mind by analysing its basic components. A key assumption in the theory is that conscious experience can be broken down into basic elements, much the same as a chemist identifying elements that make up a chemical compound.

The three basic states of consciousness – sensations, images and affections.

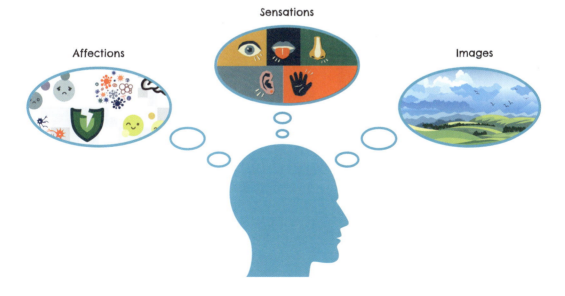

Hermann von Helmholtz.

Wundt and Titchener believed that by understanding these critical elements one could comprehend the working of the human mind. Key to this understanding was the process of introspection. This was the primary method used by the structuralists, which involved the examination of one's own conscious thoughts and feelings. Using a controlled and structured method, trained observers would report their sensations and feelings in response to stimuli under controlled laboratory conditions. Titchener would later categorize these into three basic states of consciousness: sensations (basic sensory inputs), images (mental depictions) and affections (emotional reactions). Structuralism viewed the mind as the sum total of these inputs and sought to analyse these elements to understand the complexities of human consciousness. However, structuralism was not concerned with the meaning or significance of the experiences. The primary goal of the approach was to describe the structure of the mind rather than understanding its function or purpose.

Both Wundt and Titchener stressed a scientific approach to researching the mind and believed that psychology could be a valid scientific discipline in its own right. Their approach was systematic and repeatable and as such was a significant departure from the philosophical approaches to understanding the mind that preceded the structuralist approach.

WUNDT AND THE FIRST PSYCHOLOGY LABORATORY

Wilhelm Wundt is the first person to be credited as a psychologist. Wundt's background was in medicine and physiology. At age 20 he began studying medicine at Heidelberg University and spent a semester studying physiology under Johannes Müller (the 'father of experimental physiology'). It was during this time that Wundt began to move away from doctoring and developed his interest in physiology. By 1856 he had gained his doctorate in medicine and had his first publication.

For the next decade Wundt worked as a research assistant at Heidelberg University under the physicist, physician and psychologist Hermann von Helmholtz (1821–94). Von Helmholtz was influential in the advances made throughout the 1850s in the understanding of sensory input such as reaction times, vision and perception. The association with Von Helmholtz was hugely influential on Wundt, and would later influence his approach to investigating psychological phenomena. In 1874 he published his groundbreaking book *Principles of Physiological Psychology*, which began as an 870-page book expanding to three volumes by the time it reached its sixth and final edition in 1908.

In 1879 Wundt established the first psychology laboratory at the Institute for Experimental Psychology at the University of Leipzig in Germany. Here he aimed to investigate thoughts and sensations and organize them into the essential inputs (elements) that make up human consciousness. This was the first serious attempt to approach psychological investigation in a scientific way using the methods and techniques derived from his research with Von Helmholtz.

ESSENTIAL PSYCHOLOGISTS

Wilhelm Wundt
Lived: 1832–1920
Origin: Germany
Known for: Introspection; voluntarism

Up until this point philosophers, most notably Immanuel Kant, had proposed that psychology would never be an objective science as it was impossible to measure the mind in an objective, mathematical way.

However, Wundt felt that the arguments of his peers were largely based on a misunderstanding of self-observation of the human condition. Wundt believed that experimental psychology had much in common with other scientific areas, particularly physics and physiology, highlighting that many of the same instruments used in these disciplines could also be used in psychological applications to measure phenomena such as time. He sought to move away from self-observation to a controlled method of introspection using systematic, controlled and repeatable observations. His argument was that we use external stimuli to modify our consciousness in what he referred to as 'modification from without'. In taking this structured approach Wundt effectively separated psychology from philosophy, and the process of organizing the mind became known as 'voluntarism'.

KEY VOCABULARY	
Objective	Eliminating personal biases, false assumptions and emotions from scientific research.
Subjective	The influence of personal beliefs, opinions and emotions when interpreting scientific data.
Structuralism	An early school of thought in psychology that sought to understand the mind by investigating its elemental components.
Introspection	The process of examining one's own thoughts, judgements, emotions and perceptions.
Empirical	Using observable and quantifiable data to research psychological phenomena.
Chronoscope	An instrument capable of measuring small time intervals.
Metronome	A device used by musicians to mark time at a selected rate.
Functionalism	A theoretical framework in psychology that stresses the adaptive value of mental processes and behaviour.

WUNDT AND INTROSPECTION

Wundt used trained observers employing carefully controlled procedures to respond to external stimuli such as a flashing light. The observers would then systematically analyse their response to the stimulus through the process of introspection. Early investigations focused on simple sensations and perceptions of time and space. At the institute researchers would experiment with ticking metronomes or flickering lights. The participants were then asked to reflect upon their experiences using the process of introspection. Often observers would remain outside of the room so as not to influence the outcome of the investigation. By employing these carefully controlled procedures, the same experience could be recreated each time and therefore the observations could be repeated and compared. Later, more complex concepts were investigated such as feelings, attention and memory.

The first investigation conducted at the institute was carried out by Dr Max Friedrich, titled 'On the duration of apperception in connection with

STRUCTURALIST THEORY >>

simple and compound sensations.' This investigated the time taken for certain psychological processes to take place. Empirical measurements were made of processes such as memory and reaction times using a chronoscope which could measure reaction speeds to 1/1,000th of a second.

Students flocked to study at the world's first dedicated psychology laboratory, peaking in 1912 with 620 students and Wundt supporting 186 PhD dissertations. Wundt guided the studies but the experiments and apparatus were mostly created by the students themselves.

TITCHENER AND STRUCTURALISM

One of these students, Edward Titchener, would prove to be particularly influential in the development of structuralism as a school of thought. Born in 1867 in Chichester, England, he attended Malvern College on a scholarship. His family had planned for him to take up a place in the clergy but Titchener's interests lay in science and in 1885 he went on to study biology. He then focused on studying psychology and became interested in the work of Wilhelm Wundt while he was studying at Oxford University. Titchener was the first to translate Wundt's *Principles of Physiological Psychology* from German to English. In 1890, unable to find work in the UK after graduating from Oxford, Titchener began studying under Wundt at Leipzig University, eventually earning his PhD in 1892.

> Early experiments involved participants being asked to report their experiences of external stimuli such as flashing lights.

ESSENTIAL PSYCHOLOGISTS

Edward Titchener
Lived: 1867–1927
Origin: United Kingdom
Known for: Structuralism

After gaining his PhD Titchener moved to Cornell University in New York and took a position as professor of psychology. It was here that he would establish the school of structuralism and he is credited with bringing the principles of introspection to the United States. However, his approach differed from his mentor, as he would apply Wundt's methods in a more stringent way to isolate the elements of consciousness. In this sense Titchener was not interested in any way about instinct or the unconscious mind and sought a purity in identifying the elemental sensations.

Titchener expanded on Wundt's methods by putting his students through a demanding process to become trained and skilled at introspection. Through this process observers would be able to isolate and report only the sensations they experienced in response to the stimuli. An effective observer could look inwardly and be able to describe the intensity and clarity of an image. In this way Titchener trained his students to look beyond their initial responses and instead describe other elements such as the tone of colour or the sensation experienced when viewing an object. For example, when looking at a picture of a bird a typical response might be to just describe it as 'green'. However, Titchener trained his students to break down their experience into specific elements, such as the tone of green or their sensation at seeing the bird. Using these methods Titchener's students began to isolate and analyse the psychological elements they had identified in their observations.

The group Titchener established became known as the 'Experimentalists' and was known for having a ban on women participating in the research. During this time many women were forbidden from studying at major universities such as Harvard and Columbia. Despite his views on women not being permitted in his group, Titchener actually oversaw the doctoral research of more women than any other male psychologist and his first doctoral student was Margaret Floy Washburn, who became the first woman to gain her PhD in psychology in 1894.

STRUCTURALIST THEORY >>

Wundt's students became skilled at isolating the different sensations they experienced and providing a detailed account of their response to a specific stimulus.

The Sound Cage Experiment

One such experiment, devised around 1900, was known as the sound cage. The observer would be fixed into a chair and their head held between clamps so that they were unable to move. Surrounding the observer's head were a series of horizontal and vertical bars. A phone receiver was placed on these bars and made a clicking noise. The observer would then try to identify the location of the receiver, relaying coordinates as to where they believed the receiver to be. In some cases, there were additional introspective processes but the experiment was largely to quantify and locate the sound. Titchener included a description of this device in his four-volume *Experimental Psychology*, the student manual of qualitative experiments, commonly known as 'Titchener's manuals'. There was even a company that marketed this device, selling the sound cage and manual as part of a $460 package deal.

The sound cage.

Titchener and his students continued to analyse the elemental sensations they had identified and began to investigate the laws that governed them. Drawing upon his scientific background in biology, Titchener next attempted to compile a 'periodic table' of psychological elements identified from the introspective observations of his students. He brought together his findings in *An Outline of Psychology*, published in 1899, where he reported more than 46,000 elementary sensations.

From his work to compile the periodic table of psychological elements, Titchener concluded that there were three basic states of consciousness:

- Sensations (basic sensory inputs)
- Images (mental depictions)
- Affections (emotional reactions)

He further suggested that these components could additionally be broken down into their individual properties which he defined as quality, intensity, duration and clearness:

- Quality – 'hot' or 'blue': distinguishes each element from the others.
- Intensity – how solid, loud, bright the sensation is.
- Duration – how the sensation progresses over time; how long it lasts.
- Clearness – role of attention in consciousness; clearer if attention is directed towards it.

ESSENTIAL PSYCHOLOGISTS

Margaret Floy Washburn
Lived: 1871–1939
Origin: United States of America
Known for: First woman to gain a PhD in psychology

As structuralism matured it also became more limited in its application. Titchener was aiming to discover how information was input into our consciousness by seeking to isolate and quantify the psychological elements that input information into the human mind. He emphasized that psychology could take a scientific approach and did much to introduce scientific rigour into the process of introspection. However, Titchener was still relying on the subjective views of his students and, despite their training, their sensory perception was ultimately based on their own conscious experience. The exclusion of women

ELEMENTARY SENSATIONS	NUMBER
Colour	Around 35,000
White to black range	600–700
Tones	About 11,000
Tastes	4 (sweet, sour, bitter, salty)
From the skin	4 (pressure, pain, warmth, cold)
From the internal organs	4 (pressure, pain, warmth, cold)
Smells	9 classes (could be thousands of individual sensations)
Total elementary sensations	46,708 plus an indeterminate range of smells

in these experiments certainly impacted the legitimacy of the research. Titchener also excluded other key areas of the human experience such as the subconscious and by modern standards the structuralist approach was flawed.

Ultimately structuralism would not survive much past Titchener's death in 1927. Functionalism had begun to emerge from the structuralist school of thought, whereby psychologists were more interested in the function of behaviour rather than individual inputs. This connected with the big ideas of the time such as Darwin's theory of evolution and how behaviours could be adapted to make an organism successful. Functionalism therefore differed from its predecessor, structuralism, in that psychologists sought to understand how different factors worked together rather than the assumption of consciousness being made up of piecemeal elements and senses. They also moved away from methods of introspection to use more objective practices. By the mid-20th century both structuralism and functionalism had been overtaken by new schools of thought such as the Gestalt movement.

The legacy of Wundt and Titchener is that they made a paradigm shift in how psychology was approached, setting the stage for psychology to become a discrete scientific discipline. The principles of systematic and repeatable studies can still be found in the DNA of modern psychological research. With the advent of machine learning and how humans interact with modern technology it may well be that the structuralist approach sees a resurgence as we try to understand the physical world around us and how we live and interact in the modern world.

Structuralism in Everyday Life

Introspection is still used today despite being one of the earliest methods used to investigate psychological phenomena. One such example of introspection being used in applied research comes from a study by Mark D. Griffiths (1994). Although there is not one single theory to explain persistent gambling, he believed that there were strong irrational mental processes that led to gambling behaviour.

The study investigated 30 regular and 30 non-regular gamblers playing on fruit machines in a British seaside arcade. Each was given £3 to gamble on the fruit machines and half were asked to think aloud as they were playing.

Using this 'thinking aloud method', participants would examine the role of skill by verbalizing their thought process using the following template:
- Do not censor your thoughts. Say everything that goes through your mind even if it seems irrelevant.
- Continue talking throughout, even if your ideas do not seem clearly structured.
- Speak clearly.
- Don't worry about speaking in complete sentences; use fragmented speech if necessary.
- Do not try to justify your thoughts.

Like Wundt and Titchener, the methods used were structured and repeatable as the process of gambling remained the same for each participant. By standardizing the instructions Griffiths also ensured that the participants were given the same information. The 'thinking aloud method' provided an introspective approach to analyse the thought patterns of the regular versus the non-regular gamblers.

The results found that regular gamblers were significantly more skill-oriented, believing that they could influence the outcome of the game.

The study also found that regular gamblers produced significantly more irrational verbalizations than non-regular gamblers, with 14 per cent of the regular gamblers making statements such as 'the machine loves me'. Conversely, non-regular gamblers were prone to making factual statements such as 'I lost the whole pound' and only 2.5 per cent making irrational statements.

While this study does not solve the central cause of pathological gambling, using an introspective method has opened a window into how we might treat compulsive behaviours associated with gambling.

The participants were asked to verbalize their thoughts as they gambled, revealing significant differences between regular and non-regular gamblers.

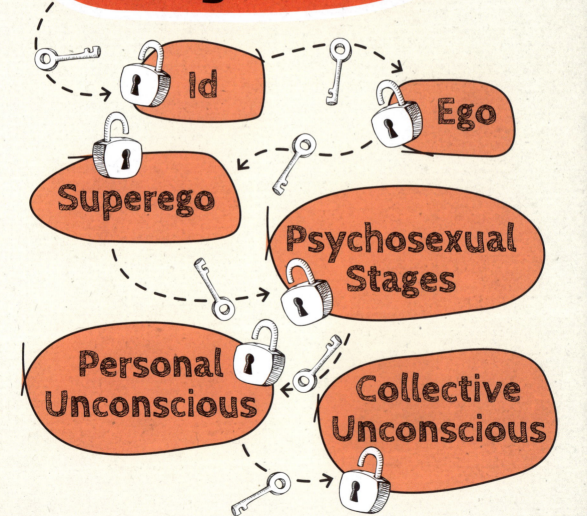

PSYCHODYNAMIC THEORY

THE FOUNDER OF THE PSYCHODYNAMIC approach to psychology, Sigmund Freud (1856–1939), is one of the most recognizable and famous figures in psychology. The psychodynamic approach is most readily associated with the work of Freud; however, it also refers to the work of his followers such as Carl Jung, Melanie Klein and Alfred Adler. What the work of these psychologists has in common is that they all propose that human behaviour is driven by forces or factors within the person.

SIGMUND FREUD

Freud embarked on his scientific career studying biology rather than psychology. He attended the University of Vienna Medical School and worked as a physician after gaining his medical degree in 1881. His biological background greatly influenced how he later interpreted psychology, believing that much of our behaviour is guided by unconscious biological urges. He also believed that our childhood experiences profoundly influenced our adult psychology, theorizing that traumatic childhood experiences could lead to mental health disorders later in life. Freud developed talking therapies that attempted to delve into a patient's unconscious mind and reveal these urges and traumas using techniques such as dream analysis.

Freud's theories are controversial as they do not match current accepted social norms in many societies. For example, Freud worked from an assumption that heterosexual relationships were the ideal and what our psyche would be striving for, and that homosexuality or any other form of sexuality was dysfunctional. He also focused largely on a male perspective, with women's drives and development being diminished or centred on their role as a potential mother. His theories are often based on his own observations of his patients and are therefore difficult to test or verify. Despite these issues Freud's work represented some of the first attempts to explain how our innate biology and childhood experiences may influence adult behaviour. His impact on the field of psychology is immeasurable and worthy of reflection.

ESSENTIAL PSYCHOLOGISTS

Sigmund Freud
Lived: 1856–1939
Origin: Austria
Known for: Psychoanalysis

<< CHAPTER 2

ASSUMPTIONS

Psychodynamic theory is a branch of psychology which assumes that our behaviour can be explained through our unconscious thoughts, feelings and desires. It assumes that childhood experiences, especially childhood trauma or conflict, influence our adult behaviours. The Freudian approach also suggests that our mind is split into three distinct parts: the id, ego and superego, also known as 'the tripartite mind'.

The psychodynamic approach assumes that all behaviour has a cause, be it biological or experiential, and therefore free will is not a consideration. This is known as 'psychic determinism'.

Sigmund Freud pioneered the approach of psychoanalysis.

KEY VOCABULARY

Psychosexual stages	The stages a child passes through from birth to around 12 years of age. According to Freud, these stages explain how our libido and sexual energy influence our development.
Tripartite mind	The three components of personality according to Freud. Includes the id, ego and superego.
Defence mechanism	A method used by the ego to protect itself from traumatic experiences or thoughts. Examples include repression and denial.
Archetype	Proposed by Carl Jung to be a set of symbols all humans are born with. They are inherited into our unconscious mind and represent the accumulated experience of humankind.
Manifest content	The content of a dream that can be remembered by a person when they awake.
Latent content	The underlying meaning of a dream and its symbols.

One of the more controversial psychosexual stages is the phallic stage which occurs between around three to six years of age. During this stage of development Freud believed that a child's libido is primarily focused on their genitals. As Freud was mainly concerned with the development of boys, he named this the 'phallic stage' after the phallus, or penis. At this stage the child may begin satisfying their libido by masturbating and may begin to notice physical differences between the sexes. If the overt suggestion that young children begin masturbating was not controversial enough, Freud also suggested that at this stage boys experience the Oedipus complex, named after the mythical Greek king Oedipus who killed his father and married his own mother. As part of the Oedipus complex boys unconsciously wish to remove and replace their father, seeing him as a rival, and focus their pleasure-seeking drives on their mother, wishing to possess her for themselves. At this stage Freud believed that boys also experienced castration anxiety, which is a fear that their father knows their unconscious desires and wishes to remove their penis, or castrate them. If a child passes through this stage and reaches a point where they identify with their same sex parent and cease to see them as a rival, then they have successfully passed through this stage of psychosexual development. Boys, for example, will imitate masculine behaviours and fulfil the male gender role.

The Oedipus myth.

A criticism of Freud's work is that it often focuses on male development but not female. Carl Jung, a student of Freud's, proposed the Electra complex to fill this gap in female development. Like Oedipus, Electra was also a mythical Greek figure in the form of a vengeful goddess. Like Electra, Jung proposed that girls develop a vengeful attitude towards their mothers. During the phallic stage they notice that while their father and/or brothers have phalluses, they and their mothers do not. They conclude that their mother must have castrated them, so they develop penis envy and become resentful towards their mother while simultaneously wishing to possess their father. For a girl to successfully pass through the phallic stage she must repress her rage towards her mother, accept that she does not have a penis, and replace her desire for a penis with the desire for a baby of her own and accept her gender role.

PSYCHODYNAMIC THEORY >> 27

FREUD'S FIVE PSYCHOSEXUAL STAGES					
Stage	Age	Focus of libido	Focus of development	Possible issues leading to fixation	Adult fixation example
Oral	0–1	Mouth, tongue, lips.	Building of trust through breastfeeding. Successfully weaning.	Trouble weaning, weaning too early or late.	Smoking, nail biting, overeating.
Anal	1–3	Anus, bowel and bladder control.	Successful potty training, learning to control bodily needs and developing a sense of independence.	Toilet training, being either too lenient or overly negative.	Anal-expulsive personality (messy, wasteful or destructive) or anal-retentive personality (obsessive orderliness).
Phallic	3–6	Genitals	Noticing biological differences between the sexes. Experiencing the Oedipus (boys) and Electra (girls) complexes.	Inability to identify with same sex parent (Freud focused on boys here).	Sexual deviancy or dysfunction.
Latency	6–12	None – libido is inactive	The balance between the biological urges (the id) and societal rules is navigated. Platonic relationships and hobbies are developed.	Lack of hobbies or healthy platonic relationships.	Immaturity and inability to develop meaningful relationships.
Genital	12+	Genitals	Sexual interest in others develops.	If all other stages were successfully completed, the person will successfully pass through this stage.	

THE TRIPARTITE MIND

Freud believed that much of what makes up our personality exists in our unconscious mind, and that it is split into three distinct parts known as the id, ego and superego. This is known as the tripartite mind. Freud also believed there is continuous conflict with each part to meet its own needs, and our behaviours are a result of balancing the needs of each part of the tripartite mind.

The tripartite mind: id, ego and superego.

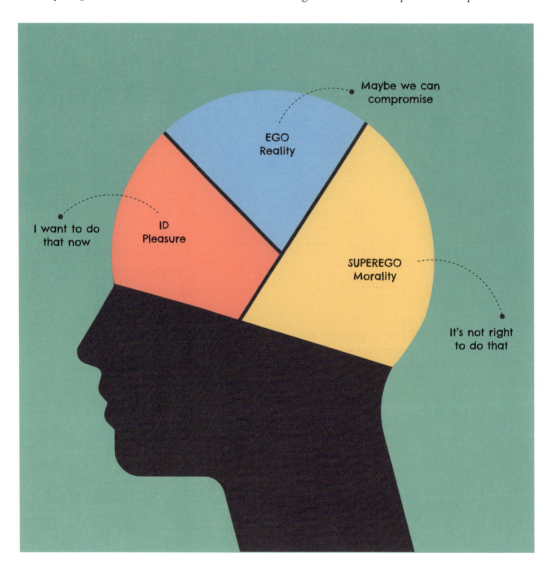

PSYCHODYNAMIC THEORY >> 29

COMMON DEFENCE MECHANISMS		
Defence mechanism	**Description**	**Example**
Denial	Denying difficult or painful events by blocking them from conscious awareness.	Ignoring symptoms of a serious illness, or not accepting that a relationship has ended.
Repression	Repressing thoughts or memories into the unconscious mind, preventing them from being consciously thought about.	Having no memory of a traumatic event that was experienced.
Projection	Projecting thoughts that we know are socially unacceptable on to another person, and attributing these thoughts to them.	Claiming that another person has been unkind to you when in fact you were unkind to them, or feeling that someone does not like you when the reality is that you do not like them.
Displacement	Satisfying an unacceptable urge by subjecting it to another object or person.	Shouting at your partner about being dissatisfied with your home when in fact you are dissatisfied with your job.
Regression	Returning to an earlier stage of development before the traumatic or troublesome event occurred.	An older child wetting the bed or sucking their thumb when overwhelmed by an event such as hospitalization of a parent.

The id is contained entirely in our unconscious mind, associated with our biological urges. It seeks immediate satisfaction, acting in response to primal urges and desires. Freud proposed that the id is present and fully developed in us from birth before we have developed our ego and superego, which would be an advantage to a newborn baby who needs to survive by obtaining resources from a parent. However, the id alone would not allow us to be a functional member of society as it knows no inhibitions.

The superego exists largely in our unconscious mind and is the last part of the tripartite mind to develop, emerging during the phallic stage in childhood as a result of interactions with our friends, family and society. It exists to moderate the pleasure-seeking urges of the id. The superego reflects the moral values of the society in which we live, acting as a conscience particularly

ESSENTIAL PSYCHOLOGISTS

Carl Jung
Lived: 1875–1961
Origin: Switzerland
Known for: Analytical Psychology

with controlling sexual urges and aggression that are forbidden by society. The superego also sets a benchmark for behaviour called 'the ideal self' that we judge ourselves against, feeling guilt and shame if we do not meet these expectations. The superego differs from the id in that it does not act entirely in the unconscious mind but can influence our conscious behaviour.

The ego is the third part of the tripartite mind and represents our conscious self. It develops from the id during infancy and mediates between the impulsive id and the real world. It also acts as a mediator between the primal urges of the id and the moral reasoning of the superego.

If all three parts of the tripartite mind are acting in harmony then a person has the potential to be psychologically healthy. If, however, either the id or superego are overactive and cannot be satisfied or mediated by the ego then a person may be psychologically unhealthy, either indulging in risky, maybe destructive, behaviours, or feeling anxiety or self-hatred.

The ego has a big job to do and can sometimes be overwhelmed with demands from the id and superego. Freud suggested that the ego protects itself in these cases using defence mechanisms that we are often unaware of.

CARL JUNG

Another important figure in the development of the psychodynamic approach was Swiss psychologist Carl Jung. Jung was considered a protégé of Freud's and the two had a very intense initial friendship which lasted around five years. Jung's work similarly emphasized the influence of the unconscious on personality. However, their relationship began to deteriorate when Jung criticized Freud's approaches, for instance his emphasis on sexuality and sexual drives being a key motivator of behaviour.

In 1912 Jung published a book titled *Psychology of the Unconscious* in which he outlined his own theories of psychology and first introduced his concept of analytical psychology. Jung believed like Freud that the human psyche was split into three parts; however, he proposed the ego, the personal unconscious, and the collective unconscious.

For Jung, the ego represents the conscious experience of a person. This includes their memories, thoughts and emotions.

The personal and collective unconscious both reside in the unconscious mind. Jung believed that the personal unconscious contained forgotten or repressed memories and complexes. A complex is a cluster of feelings, memories and thoughts associated with a specific emotional theme or

Carl Jung developed the concept of the collective unconscious.

concept and the more elements there are to the cluster, the more influence that complex has on a person. We develop complexes through troubling experiences or unresolved conflicts. For example, an inferiority complex may stem from a sense of inadequacy and therefore lead to social withdrawal, or a power complex may stem from feelings of vulnerability but display itself as obsession with dominance and control. While this definition of complexes makes them appear maladaptive, Jung did also propose that complexes can conceal strengths in our personality, and understanding them may give us a gateway into our deeper unconscious, the collective unconscious.

Jung proposed that the collective unconscious was imprinted on the brain at birth. It is a set of 'primordial images' that we inherit from our ancestors and remain latent in the brain. Jung had a vast knowledge of folklore and mythologies, and he claimed that the concept of a collective unconscious could explain why the themes of certain legends are repeated in cultures all over the world. He also applied this concept to explain new scientific discoveries. For example, when hearing that during a trip across the South Seas the physician Robert Mayer had answered a question of physics and discovered the concept of conservation of energy, Jung was excited to learn that the idea had seemingly come to Mayer unbidden. Jung proposed that, 'The idea of energy and of its conservation must be a primordial image that lay dormant in the absolute unconscious.' Jung called these psychological symbols and themes 'archetypes'.

The psychodynamic approach pioneered by Sigmund Freud remains influential in our understanding of human behaviour and personality. It has been so widely received that the language used to describe his approach has become commonplace in society. We will often hear the word 'ego' being used to describe how a person behaves or to describe their personality type. Central to Freud's psychodynamic approach was the relationship between the unconscious and conscious mind which he believed was shaped in our childhood. Freud conceptualized these as separate parts which he called the id, ego and superego. However, some psychologists were beginning to take an alternative view that the mental processes and behaviour were too complex to be broken down into individual sensory elements or the conscious and unconscious parts of the mind. Instead they viewed the human experience as being more holistic and that our perception of the world was greater than the sum of all the individual inputs we encounter in our lives.

Psychodynamic Approaches in Everyday Life: Dream Analysis

Therapies that are influenced by the psychodynamic approach involve using techniques such as dream analysis or word association to delve into the patient's unconscious mind and bring to their conscious attention feelings, desires or experiences that may be causing them poor mental health in the present.

Dream analysis involves using what a patient remembers about their dreams (known as 'manifest content') to help uncover their unconscious thoughts by finding the hidden meaning of that aspect of their dream (latent content).

Freud believed that these unconscious thoughts and desires may have originated in the id and been suppressed by the ego and superego, or they may be traumatic memories that we are being protected from by an ego defence mechanism. When we sleep, the ego's defences are lowered and we may be more able to access these fears or desires. Jung also championed dream analysis, believing that rather than dreams representing unhealthy urges or desires they were in fact a way for our unconscious to bring to our attention issues we needed to address. Freud did not propose a universal set of symbols that have a similar meaning across all dreams and the concept of a dream dictionary is in opposition to the purpose of dream analysis. Each feature of a dream has an individual meaning for each person based on their personal experiences. Rather than attempt to decode a patient's dreams himself, Freud would use additional techniques such as free association to encourage the patient to uncover the hidden meaning in their dream themself.

Free association involves a patient discussing freely the thoughts that come to the forefront of their mind. The therapist might introduce a word or concept and ask that the patient discuss whatever comes to mind first.

Dream analysis is still used by therapists but is not common, mainly used by psychoanalysts to uncover themes for discussion when working with patients.

Dream analysis.

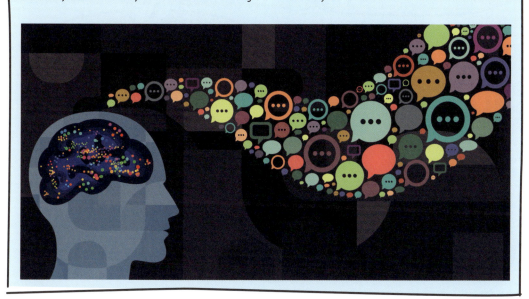

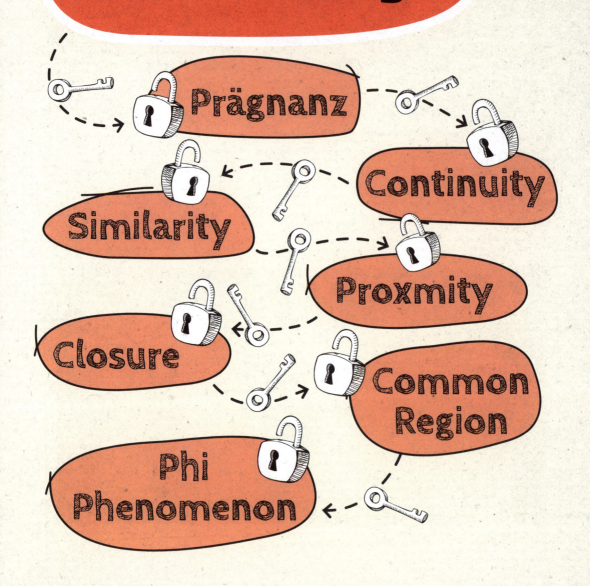

GESTALT PSYCHOLOGY is a school of thought that appeared in Germany in the early 20th century in response to structuralism and functionalism. Gestalt is a German word that loosely translates as to have form, to take shape or the whole. Gestalt theory explores how people experience and perceive the world around them, emphasizing that the whole of anything is greater than the sum of all its parts.

ESSENTIAL PSYCHOLOGISTS

Max Wertheimer
Lived: 1880–1943
Origin: Austria-Hungary
Known for: Gestalt Psychology

The origins of the Gestalt school of thought can be traced to three prominent psychologists: Max Wertheimer (1880–1943), Wolfgang Köhler (1887–1967) and Kurt Koffka (1886–1941). They were interested in how people instinctively organize their experiences and the natural processes underlying our perceptions of the world. They proposed that the human mind perceives the world holistically as meaningful patterns and configurations rather than individual inputs or elements. This approach provided the foundation for the modern study of perception and was a significant departure from structuralism, which sought to break down human experience into the most basic elementary sensations.

ASSUMPTIONS

The principles of Gestalt psychology are founded upon how the mind tends to find order in disorder and that human perception takes place in the mind rather than just the elemental sensations that the brain receives. Therefore human perception of the world around us is about how we make sense of these inputs and is based on predictable patterns that can be influenced by our motivations and experience of the world. In 1923 Max Wertheimer established the key principles of Gestalt psychology:

Prägnanz

Also known as 'the law of simplicity'. This describes how the human mind seeks to perceive complex and ambiguous inputs in their simplest form. A good example of this is how we perceive the Olympic logo. We tend to see this in a simplistic form where there are five coloured circles. However, if you look closely you start to see how the rings interconnect in an intricate pattern of curves, perspective and colour.

The Olympic rings appear at first to be five coloured rings. Look closer and you will see that they are a more intricate design than first appears.

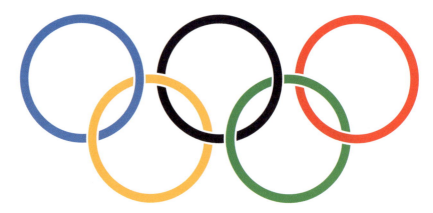

Continuity

This states that the human mind will organize elements positioned in a line or a curve and will perceive these as being related to one another. Elements that are not positioned in a line or curved pattern will be perceived as separate entities.

The Coca-Cola logo is a good example of the law of continuity. Our eye is drawn along the text connecting the words together.

GESTALT THEORY >>   37

Similarity

This Gestalt law suggests that we group items together depending on factors such as their shape, colour, size, orientation and texture. For example, we would group vehicles depending on their size and shape and might categorize some as small cars, some as family-sized cars or maybe even trucks if they are particularly large.

A traffic jam shows how we group objects together. Look into the distance and you see traffic or vehicles. In the foreground you can see distinct vehicles of different types such as cars, vans and lorries.

Proximity

The principle of proximity states that objects or elements located in close proximity to one another are perceived as a whole. The Girl Scouts logo is a good example of how our mind constructs the image of three faces from a series of shapes in close proximity.

The Girl Scouts logo shows three faces when we perceive the whole due to the proximity of the shape and tone of the logo.

Closure

This principle suggests that the human brain will tend to infill gaps in space to create shapes and form in what the mind is perceiving. Where there is missing information we will infill shapes, colour and pattern to bring stability to what we are seeing. An example of where we might do this is looking at the World Wide Fund for Nature (WWF) symbol. This is a simple image with black and white shapes and no outline for the head or body of the bear. Our brain infills the missing information to create the image of a panda bear which is so closely associated with the conservation work of the WWF.

Look closely at the image. It is a collection of black and white shapes, yet we can clearly see the image of a panda bear despite there being no outline to the image.

Common Region

This principle proposes that objects contained in the same closed space such as a box or a circle will be perceived as being related to one another. This may well override other laws such as the principle of proximity. This principle is commonly applied on social media platforms where information is grouped together in boxes.

Social media platforms use the common region principle to clearly present data and information.

Gestalt Psychology in Everyday Life: Design

Gestalt theory is used by designers and artists to create visually compelling artwork and images to fascinate and draw our attention. The ideas are drawn from the laws of Gestalt such as proximity and closure (as discussed earlier in this chapter) using empty space and colour to create an optical illusion of shape and form.

Designers and artists at the Bauhaus, an early 20th century German experimental art school, investigated the principles of Gestalt in their teaching and personal projects. Subsequently artists and designers have referred to the principles of Gestalt to reduce the complexity of images and group components to form a recognizable image.

Perhaps one of the most common places we experience Gestalt principles is in branding and marketing techniques. Designers will create distinctive logos often using the laws set out by Max Wertheimer, Wolfgang Köhler and Kurt Koffka. The law of continuity can be seen in the Coca-Cola wording, whereas the law of closure has been applied to the image of the panda bear in the WWF logo. Using these techniques designers can create a brand image that we instantly recognize.

Gestalt principles are also commonly used in the design of social media platforms. Using the common region principle, information is often placed in a box or a coloured shape to separate the information from the background. This is done so that we visually attain the advertising or marketing information of the products that are being promoted to us.

The Bauhaus school of art and design.

THE NATURE OF OPTICAL ILLUSION

Max Wertheimer was born in Prague in 1880. Initially he studied law at the University of Prague but his interests lay in physiology, philosophy and psychology and he began studying these subjects in 1901 at the University of Berlin. He earned his doctorate from the University of Würzburg in 1904, developing a lie detector based on word association, for applications in law. According to legend he became interested in perception on a train journey during the summer of 1910. Some accounts say that he was playing with a children's toy whereas others state that it was alternating signal lights flashing past the train that inspired him. Whatever it was that caught his attention it led to Wertheimer making a simple yet important observation. Wertheimer noted that stationary objects shown in fast succession could be perceived as moving. When he arrived in Frankfurt he purchased a toy stroboscope and began experimenting with his ideas around apparent motion in his hotel room. Wertheimer later contacted Wolfgang Köhler, who at this time was working as a lab assistant at the University of Frankfurt. Köhler provided lab space and a rotating wheel called a tachistoscope which was specially constructed at the university to observe successive images and investigate the nuances of apparent movement.

In 1912 Wertheimer formalized his observation in a paper titled 'Experimental Studies of the Perception of Movement'. This paper explored the nature of optical illusion and human perception of movement, and noted how we can perceive movement when no actual motion has taken place. Wertheimer would later go on to call this optical illusion phi phenomenon. An example of this is where a series of still images changes rapidly in front of our eyes and we perceive these images as being in motion. In fact the methods of generating an apparent movement had been used by the film industry and the properties of this optical illusion discerned more than 60 years before Wertheimer published his paper.

Wertheimer's observation was important as the phi phenomenon could not be explained by approaches such as the structuralist view that the senses perceive the world piecemeal. By varying the colour, intensity and distances between objects under experimental conditions, Wertheimer could show that conventional theories to explain observed motion were incorrect. Gestalt psychology argued that it was reductive to explain the illusion of apparent movement as the product of individual sensory elements. Instead the Gestalt approach argued that the individual's nervous system assimilates the input, in this case a series of images, through many sensory experiences

KEY VOCABULARY

Stroboscope	An instrument for determining speeds of rotation or studying periodic motion by beaming a bright light at intervals so that a moving or rotating object appears stationary.
Tachistoscope	An instrument used for exposing objects to the eye for a very brief, measured period of time.
Phi phenomenon	An illusion of movement whereby two objects in close proximity are presented in quick succession.
Structuralism	An early school of thought in psychology that sought to understand the mind by investigating its elemental components.
Gestalt	A school of thought in psychology where the organized whole that is perceived is greater than the sum of all its parts.
Gestalt Therapy	A humanistic, holistic, person-centred form of psychotherapy that is focused on a person's present life and challenges rather than examining past experiences.

at the same time. Therefore the observed movement results from an image instantaneously constructed in the mind rather than through individual inputs. In this way the mind is tricked into seeing a continuous movement where there is in fact no movement of the images. Gestalt (loosely translated as 'the whole' or 'to have form') therefore sees the apparent movement as being greater than the sum of the individual sensory inputs. The phi phenomenon results from the mind perceiving the 'whole' and placing structure and form on what is being experienced to make sense of the world around us. This principle would be later established as the 'Law of Prägnanz' and would become a founding principle of Gestalt psychology.

WOLFGANG KÖHLER'S MENTALITY OF APES

Of the Gestalt psychologists, perhaps the best known is Wolfgang Köhler. He is known for extending the application of Gestalt psychology beyond sensory experience, to investigate intelligence and behaviour in apes. In 1913 the Royal Prussian Academy of Sciences (Berlin) founded the Anthropoid Station for psychological and physiological research in chimpanzees and other apes on the island of Tenerife. Köhler was the second and final director of the station which researched natural behaviours, such as body language exhibited by the animals. At the outbreak of World War I Köhler was marooned in the Canary Islands and carried out a series of studies, which would become classics in comparative psychology, investigating intelligent behaviour in chimpanzees. They would also form the basis of his book, *Intelligenzprüfungen an Menschenaffen* (The Mentality of Apes), published in 1921.

His studies involved nine chimpanzees and used the equipment left in the station including boxes, sticks and a few pens. Using these he constructed a variety of tasks that the chimps had to perform to obtain food that was initially inaccessible to them. For example, a simple barrier would be placed between the chimp and the food. It had been observed that in cats and dogs they became fixated on the food behind the barrier and had not moved away or gone around the barrier to find the food. However, the chimps' problem-solving was found to be more creative and they would immediately circumvent the barrier to acquire the food. Route planning was not unique to the chimps; it was rather that cats and dogs used trial and error to overcome the barriers and mazes set by Köhler, whereas the chimpanzees appeared to problem-solve using insight and planning.

In other tests Köhler would use a wire to suspend fruit, such as bananas, above the chimpanzee enclosure. Objects such as boxes and poles along with some of the chimps' toys were placed in proximity to the hanging fruit. Some of the studies were filmed. Initially the chimps can be seen to be jumping up to try and reach the fruit. This would usually result in them becoming frustrated and angry as the fruit remained out of reach. The chimpanzees would walk away and after a period of time reflecting on the problem, they would gather the objects in the enclosure and begin using them to try and obtain the food. Their solutions to the problem would also vary. One chimpanzee would use a method of stacking several boxes and can be seen repeatedly trying to balance the boxes until they were high enough to climb up and reach the fruit. Another chimp called Sultan was observed to join two sticks together in order to knock the bananas to the ground. More recent studies at the Max Planck Institute have shown that apes can even use water to solve abstract problems to obtain food. What appears to be common in these attempts to problem-solve, is the chimps' ability to use insight and to experiment in their mind before they use the objects as tools to get the food.

The apes' ability to see relationships between objects and stimuli reinforced the assumptions of the Gestalt approach, that perception and behaviour cannot be explained by individual sensory input alone but results from multiple factors. Köhler's experiments with the apes appeared to support this view as they had shown insight, planning and a degree of creative problem-solving, all interacting together to obtain the food. Wertheimer, Köhler, Koffka and their students extended the ideas of the Gestalt approach beyond perception to other areas such as problem-solving, learning and thinking.

With World War II on the horizon, Köhler became a staunch critic of Adolf Hitler's government and left for the United States in 1935, becoming professor of psychology at Swarthmore University, Pennsylvania until 1955. Similarly, Max Wertheimer escaped from Germany in 1933 and became professor at the New School for Social Research in New York City and he spent the rest of his life there. Kurt Koffka moved to the United States earlier in the 1920s and remained there until his death in 1941. He was largely responsible for spreading

ESSENTIAL PSYCHOLOGISTS

Wolfgang Köhler
Lived: 1887–1967
Origin: Germany
Known for: Gestalt Psychology

<< CHAPTER 3

Sultan the chimpanzee at Köhler's research station in Tenerife.

the Gestalt approach outside of Germany. In later years, the Gestalt principles would be applied to areas such as personality development and social psychology, developing the Gestalt approach far beyond its origins in perception of movement. Though Gestalt did not survive as a distinct school of psychology much beyond the 1950s it made important contributions in understanding how the world around us is perceived by the mind and that perception of the whole may be greater than the sum of all the parts that construct our reality.

GESTALT THERAPY

Gestalt therapy is a therapeutic approach concerned with present experience and encourages taking responsibility rather than placing blame on upbringing. Although not directly connected to the original ideas of Gestalt, this therapeutic approach focuses on understanding the 'whole' context of an individual and the challenges they experience.

Gestalt therapy was developed in the USA in the 1940s most notably by Friedrich S. Perls (1893–1970) and his wife Laura Perls (1905–1990). Laura Perls summed up the development of Gestalt therapy as changing the historical, almost archaeological, Freudian viewpoint and as moving away from the piecemeal arguments of the structuralist approach. Gestalt therapy therefore had a holistic approach and focused on explicit awareness of the 'here' and 'now'.

ESSENTIAL PSYCHOLOGISTS

Kurt Koffka
Lived: 1886–1941
Origin: Germany
Known for: Gestalt Psychology

CHAPTER 3

Gestalt therapy
tries to understand
the whole and
focuses on the here
and now.

The practice emphasizes cognitive understanding of the patient's current experiences and encourages the individual to use mindfulness to achieve satisfaction in areas of their life that may have been previously blocked. Gestalt therapy uses a creative approach and includes several techniques (see below).

For people being treated by Gestalt therapy it can offer a route to improved self-awareness and better emotional regulation. Although the benefits of Gestalt therapy are not fully supported by evidence, the approach has useful applications in treating anxiety, depression and issues around self-esteem.

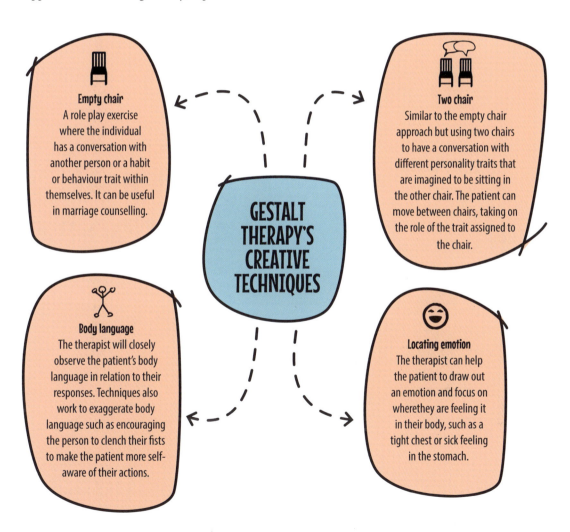

GESTALT THERAPY'S CREATIVE TECHNIQUES

Empty chair
A role play exercise where the individual has a conversation with another person or a habit or behaviour trait within themselves. It can be useful in marriage counselling.

Two chair
Similar to the empty chair approach but using two chairs to have a conversation with different personality traits that are imagined to be sitting in the other chair. The patient can move between chairs, taking on the role of the trait assigned to the chair.

Body language
The therapist will closely observe the patient's body language in relation to their responses. Techniques also work to exaggerate body language such as encouraging the person to clench their fists to make the patient more self-aware of their actions.

Locating emotion
The therapist can help the patient to draw out an emotion and focus on where they are feeling it in their body, such as a tight chest or sick feeling in the stomach.

Chapter 4
Behaviourism

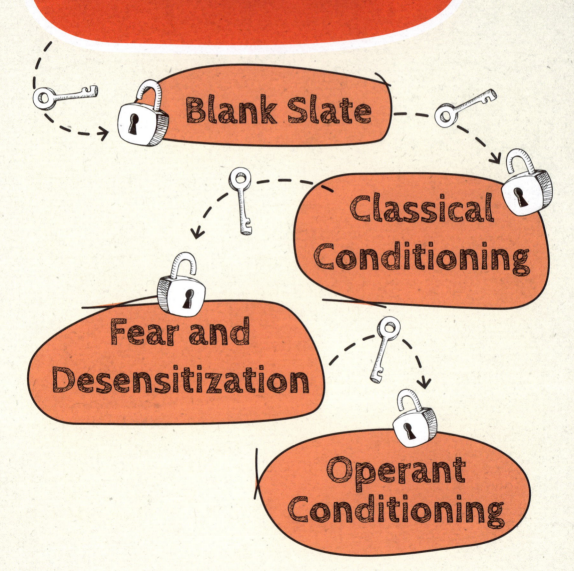

BEHAVIOURISM, also known as 'behavioural psychology', emerged in the early 20th century and is often considered to be a reaction to the subjective methods popularized by the psychologists of the psychodynamic approach. By contrast, psychologists following the behavioural approach use empirical, measurable methods to investigate cause and effect in human behaviour. What is happening in the mind, what cannot be seen or measured in between this cause and effect, would not be a focus for behavioural psychologists.

A pioneer of this approach, John B. Watson, stated that 'Psychology, as the behaviourist views it, is a purely objective, experimental branch of natural science which needs introspection as little as do the sciences of chemistry and physics'. This approach sought to give psychology its place among the traditional sciences through rigorous and well controlled experimentation.

ESSENTIAL PSYCHOLOGISTS

John Broadus Watson
Lived: 1878–1958
Origin: United States of America
Known for: Methodological Behaviourism

ASSUMPTIONS

Behaviourism emphasizes the importance of the environment on human behaviour, assuming that humans are born as a 'blank slate' ready for their experiences in the world to shape their behaviour. This learning occurs through mechanisms such as classical conditioning or operant conditioning which will be discussed in more detail during this chapter.

This approach also assumes that humans and animals learn in similar ways, so research conducted on animal learning can in turn be applied to the psychology of human behaviour.

Behaviourism itself can be subdivided into several distinct areas, one being methodological

KEY VOCABULARY

Classical conditioning	A type of learning that takes place when a neutral stimulus (e.g. a metronome) is repeatedly paired with an unconditioned stimulus (e.g. food) which elicits an unconditioned response (salivating), until the response becomes conditioned to be elicited by the now conditioned stimulus (e.g. the metronome alone elicits salivation).
Stimulus	Any object, event or situation that elicits a response from an organism. In classical conditioning this can be an unconditioned stimulus that naturally elicits a response (e.g. food causing salivation), a neutral stimulus which elicits no specific response (e.g. a metronome), or a conditioned stimulus which is what a neutral stimulus becomes after repeated pairings with an unconditioned stimulus (e.g. a metronome causing salivation).
Response	A reaction to a stimulus. This may be a reflex action such as salivating in the presence of food or a behavioural reaction such as pressing a lever when a specific shape is seen.
Unconditioned	Naturally occurring and unlearned. For example, an unconditioned stimulus may be food or a loud noise; an unconditioned response may be to salivate in the presence of food or a baby crying when they hear a loud noise.
Conditioned	Behaviour occurring as a result of experience or learning. For example, classical and operant conditioning.
Operant conditioning	A type of learning that takes place when a behaviour is associated with a consequence. The type of consequence will cause the behaviour to be either more likely to be repeated or less likely to be repeated.
Reinforcement	A consequence of an action that makes the action more likely to be repeated. Can be labelled as positive (adding) or negative (taking away). For example, positive reinforcement may be giving a child sweets for displaying desirable behaviour; negative reinforcement may be a seatbelt alarm that stops making a noise once the seatbelt is plugged in.
Punishment	A consequence of an action that makes the action less likely to be repeated. Can be labelled as positive (adding) or negative (taking away).

BEHAVIOURISM

ESSENTIAL PSYCHOLOGISTS

Ivan Pavlov
Lived: 1849–1936
Origin: Russia
Known for: Classical Conditioning

behaviourism which was favoured by Watson. This approach proposes that behaviour can be studied without reference to any mental processes such as thoughts, feelings or intentions. The focus is upon the relationship between a stimulus in the environment and the behavioural response to that stimulus. One of the most famous pieces of research in this area was not conducted by a psychologist, but by a Russian physiologist called Ivan Pavlov.

PAVLOV AND CLASSICAL CONDITIONING

Pavlov did not originally set out to study the phenomenon we now call classical conditioning. He was in fact studying the digestive systems of dogs by measuring the saliva they produced when presented with food. Salivating is a reflex action, so not something the dogs can consciously control, and the food was the stimulus that caused the reflex action. The relationship between stimulus and response is important when understanding the mechanisms of classical conditioning.

What Pavlov noticed was that the dogs did not only salivate when they were presented with their food, they also salivated when they were aware of other stimuli that were associated with the delivery of their food, such as seeing Pavlov's research assistants.

Pavlov decided to study this phenomenon systematically. He asked his assistants to present the dogs with the unconditioned stimulus of food, which they naturally reacted to with the unconditioned response of

<< CHAPTER 4

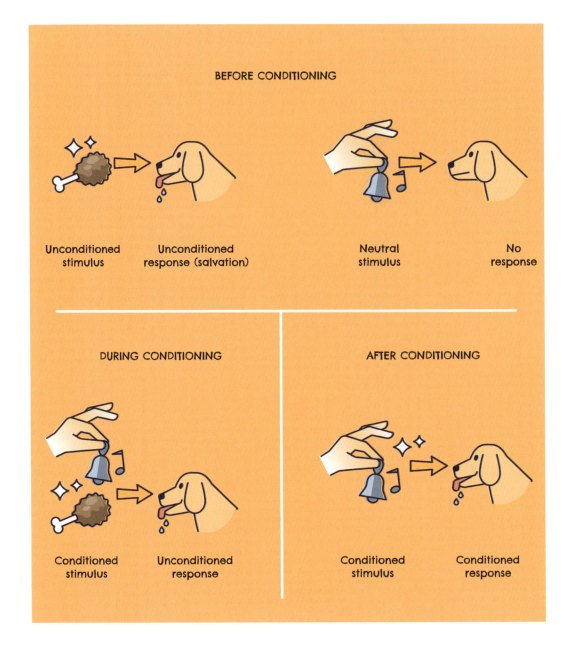

Classical conditioning.

salivating. He then asked his assistants to begin a metronome clicking at the same time as they presented the food.

In classical conditioning we say that the naturally occurring stimuli and response are 'unconditioned' because the association between them has not been deliberately conditioned (or trained) by the investigator. The new stimulus, in this case the metronome, is known as a 'neutral stimulus' because the animal or person being studied has a neutral, or no, response to that stimulus at the start of the study.

This process was repeated until Pavlov observed that the dogs had begun to associate the sound of the metronome, which was now a conditioned stimulus, with the presence of food. Next, Pavlov and his assistants presented the dogs with only the metronome and observed that they began to display a new conditioned response of salivating when presented with the metronome, even without the presence of food. The dogs had been successfully conditioned to associate the metronome with food.

We can observe and experience the effects of classical conditioning in our everyday lives. Have you ever heard someone else's phone bleep with the same tone as your own, and instinctively reached for your phone? This could be the result of classical conditioning. Researchers have even found that habitual coffee drinkers show a conditioned response linked to caffeine. Just the sight and smell of coffee caused the habitual consumers to have quicker reaction times, and the more often they drank coffee, the greater the effect was. Without originally intending to, Pavlov unlocked a fundamental mechanism of how we learn through association, and therefore how our behaviour can be influenced by our environment.

CONDITIONING FEAR

While many studies concerning conditioning such as Pavlov's are conducted on animals, there are some which use human subjects. One of the most controversial was conducted by John B. Watson and Rosalie Raynor.

Often called the 'Little Albert' study, this research is actually entitled 'Conditioned emotional reactions' and was published in *The Journal of Experimental Psychology* in 1920.

Watson and Raynor recruited a nine-month-old boy who was named in the study as 'Albert B'. He was the child of a nurse at the hospital in which

Watson and Raynor were working and his mother agreed to him taking part, a decision which may now seem surprising considering the response that Watson and Raynor were planning to condition in Albert. Watson and Raynor then spent the next three months attempting to condition a fear of rats in Albert with the promise that they would reverse any conditioning before concluding the study.

A summary of their procedures is outlined below:

Emotional tests 9 months old	Albert was presented with a variety of objects to see how he naturally responded to them. The objects included animals such as a white rat, a rabbit, a dog and a monkey. He did not seem to react fearfully to any of the animals or items presented.
Session 1 Establishing a conditioned emotional response 11 months 3 days old	Watson and Raynor began presenting Albert with a white rat, then banging a bar loudly behind his head whenever he reached out to touch the rat. This was intended to condition a fear response in Albert by teaching him to associate the unconditioned stimulus of the rat with an unconditioned response of shock or fear caused by the loud noise. They repeated these procedures twice.
Session 2 Testing the conditioned emotional response 11 months 10 days old	A week later Albert was presented with the rat again but this time with no loud sound being presented with it. He reached out carefully to touch the rat, but then drew his hand back. Watson and Raynor gave him other things to play with and he played happily, showing that he had not simply become fearful of any object given to him by them. He had apparently associated the rat with an unpleasant response and avoided touching it.
Session 3 Generalization 11 months 15 days old	Watson and Raynor presented Albert with other fluffy animals and objects, including a white rat and a rabbit which he appeared fearful of. He was less fearful of a dog and a fur coat, and showed no fear of cotton wool or Watson's hair! This suggests that he had generalized his fear of the white rat on to other small mammals such as the rabbit, but not all animals and furry objects.

BEHAVIOURISM >> 57

Session 4 Changing the environment 11 months 20 days old	At this stage Albert's conditioning was refreshed by associating the rat with the loud noise a few more times. Watson and Raynor then took Albert to a large bright room quite different to the one that they had previously been using (a small 'dark room' usually used to develop X-rays). This was to test whether he would show the same response in a new environment, or whether his conditioning only had an effect in the original environment in which it was learned. They presented him again with the animals and objects from session 3 and found that while he still responded to the rat and rabbit fearfully, it was a less strong response than it had been in the original room.
Session 5 The effect of time 12 months 21 days old	Watson and Raynor let a month pass with no conditioning taking place or being refreshed, then tested Albert again. They found that his responses were still present, but again they were less strong than they had been previously.

Soon after Watson and Raynor's final session with Albert his mother left the hospital, taking him with her. They were never able to conclude their studies and attempt to reverse Albert's conditioning. While attempts have been made to find the true identity of Albert it is not conclusively known whether this early conditioning had a long-term effect on his behaviour. However unethical and therefore unjustified this study may seem today, the thorough procedures and intricate documenting of each stage by Watson and Raynor, which even included video recordings, provide strong evidence that children may learn fear responses through conditioning in childhood. This could in turn explain some of our phobias in adulthood. For example, a child growing up with a parent who panics and screams every time they see a spider may be conditioned to associate this unpleasant sound and feeling with spiders, and therefore grow to be fearful of spiders themselves.

Although Watson and Raynor did not get the chance to reverse Albert's conditioning, research such as theirs has helped psychologists to understand the mechanisms of how fear can be conditioned, and therefore how to undo

The Little Albert experiment

that conditioning. Systematic desensitization, for example, uses similar techniques to classical conditioning. However, instead of experiencing a conditioned fear response when presented with a fearful stimulus – be that an animal, object or situation – the patient is conditioned to associate feelings of calm and relaxation with that stimulus. By gradually building up the patient's exposure to their fear stimulus and encouraging them to use relaxation techniques while doing so, a new conditioned response can be associated with the fearful stimulus.

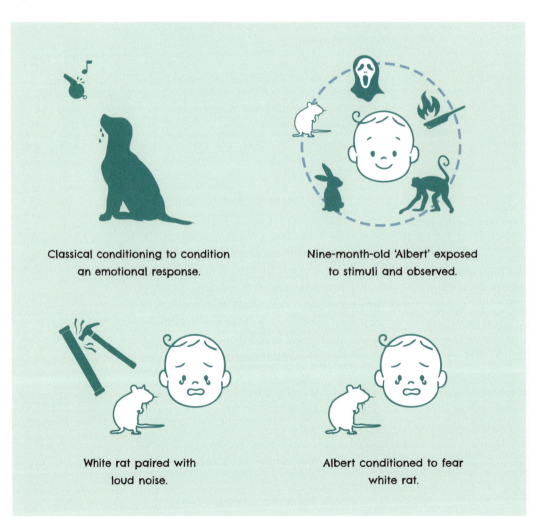

Classical conditioning to condition an emotional response.

Nine-month-old 'Albert' exposed to stimuli and observed.

White rat paired with loud noise.

Albert conditioned to fear white rat.

SKINNER AND OPERANT CONDITIONING

In contrast to the methodological approach to behaviourism that we have been discussing is the radical behaviourism pioneered by B. F. Skinner. This approach also proposes that our behaviour is caused by external influences, but rather than simply observing a stimulus and response relationship it also considers our private thoughts and feelings to play a role in shaping that response. For example, our private, internal reaction to punishment and reward.

While working at Harvard in the 1930s Skinner investigated the concept of operant conditioning. To study the effect of reward and punishments on learning in animals he developed a box which contained a stimulus (such as light, an image or a sound) and a lever which an animal could press to receive a reward, which would act as reinforcement. It also contained an electrified floor which could give a mild but unpleasant electric shock to act as a punishment. Skinner and his students could then present the animal with a stimulus such as an image or sound which indicated that the animal should press the lever or key to receive reinforcement in the form of a food pellet. If they pressed the lever when they were not supposed to they may receive a punishment in the form of an electric shock.

Through this schedule of reinforcements and punishments the animal would learn when the 'correct' time was to press the lever. Skinner was attempting to demonstrate that learning occurred not simply through the stimulus and response relationship, but also through what occurred after the response of pressing the lever, be it a reinforcement or a punishment.

Skinner also discovered that other factors could influence how successful this simple method of learning could be. He found that if an animal was rewarded every time they pressed the lever then they soon grew bored of the behaviour and their response became 'extinct'. They stopped reacting to the stimulus. In follow-up studies Skinner tried giving rewards on a fixed ratio, for example after every five lever presses, or a fixed interval, meaning the animal only received their reward after a certain amount of time had passed. However, the most successful ratio that he found was a variable ratio, whereby the animal received their reinforcement after a random number of responses.

ESSENTIAL PSYCHOLOGISTS

Burrhus Frederic Skinner
Lived: 1904–90
Origin: United States of America
Known for: Operant Conditioning

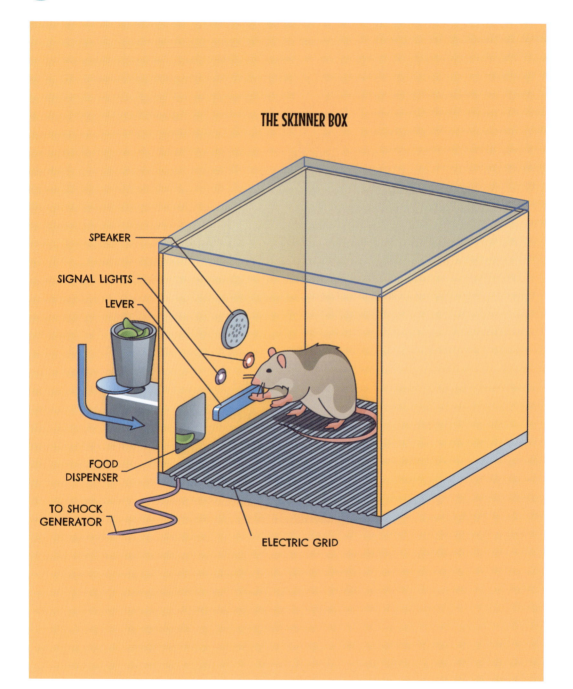

Behaviourism in Everyday Life: Gambling and Animal Training

Gambling

We see Skinner's discovery of the effect of a variable ratio of reinforcement being used to the advantage of casino owners, where gambling machines operate on a variable ratio of rewards. You pull the lever, and every now and then at unpredictable intervals you receive a reward, so you try again, and again.

Animal training

In dog training, owners are taught to use a variety of different treats when training their dogs. If you are training your dog to return to you to receive a treat, but you always use the dog's favourite treat, why should they return every time? Maybe that squirrel is more interesting than the treat, and they know they will get the treat next time anyway. But with a variety of treats on offer the dog does not know whether or not when you call them this time they may receive that much-loved special treat, and if they don't come back now will the opportunity have passed?

While behavioural psychology provides us with useful insights into the mechanisms of learning and behaviour, it does not reveal the underlying mental processes involved. That is the job of cognitive psychology, the subject of our next chapter.

Giving a dog a treat as a reward for good behaviour is an example of classical conditioning in action.

Chapter 5
Cognitive Psychology

COGNITIVE PSYCHOLOGY

Since the time of Plato and Aristotle we see evidence of people theorizing about the nature of the mind and thought, but it is not until the cognitive revolution of the 1950s and 60s that the cognitive approach emerged as a distinct branch of the relatively new science of psychology. This approach refuted the view of behavioural psychology that internal mental processes are unknowable, and aimed to look 'inside the black box' of the mind. Cognitive psychologists aimed to study the processes between the stimulus and response relationships proposed by the behavioural approach.

ASSUMPTIONS

The cognitive approach assumes that the mind works like a computer. It receives input, processes that input, and then produces an output in the form of a behavioural response.

The approach also acknowledges that internal mental processes influence our behaviour. This is the 'process' part of the computer analogy. Four well-known examples include:

- Perception – how we perceive the features of an animal such as a bird.
- Attention – how we attain the features that we think might be important.
- Memory – how we search our memory for similar features we have seen before, such as wings.
- Language – finally using language to label the creature we see as a bird.

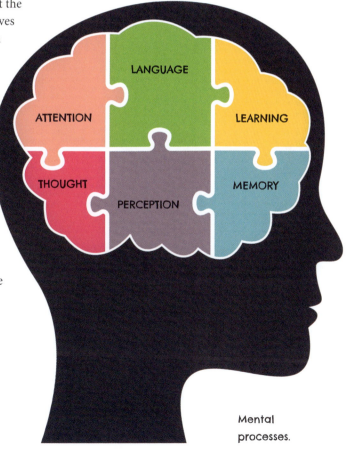

Mental processes.

<< CHAPTER 5

The concept of schemas are also integral to this approach. Schemas are organized packets of information that we build up through experience and are stored in our long-term memory. For example, as a child we may first develop a schema for birds as being animals with wings, but as we experience more interactions with our environment we learn that bats are not birds but they do also have wings. So we build a new schema for birds, for example animals with wings and a beak.

The multi-store model of memory is a good application of these cognitive assumptions. It suggests that we receive input from our surroundings which we pay attention to, this is then processed by our short-term and long-term memory stores, and the output is that we remember this input at a later date.

The multi-store model of memory.

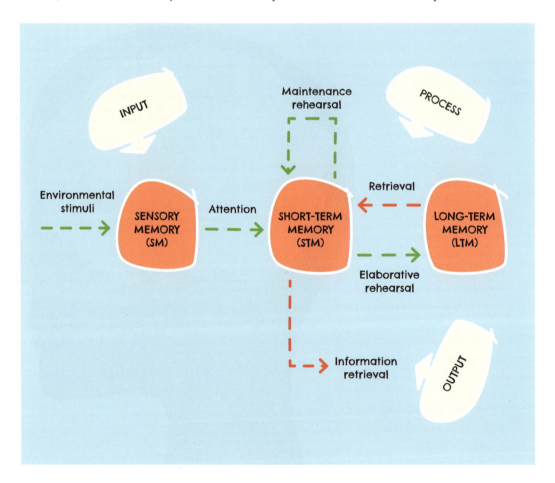

KEY VOCABULARY	
Internal mental processes	Operations that occur in the mind such as perception, memory and attention. Also known as 'mediational processes' as they occur between the stimulus and response that are experienced by a person.
Schema	A collection of basic knowledge about an object or concept that serves as a guide for understanding. For example, a child's schema for a bird may be an animal with wings, feathers and a beak.
Assimilation	Absorbing and adding new information into a schema.
Accommodation	Adjusting a schema based on new information.
Cognitive behavioural therapy	A form of therapy that aims to help a patient using a process known as 'cognitive restructuring'. The therapist and patient identify maladaptive thought processes and replace them with more functional processes.

SHORT-TERM MEMORY

In 1966 British psychologist Alan Baddeley attempted to study memory processes inside the 'black box' of the mind. He set out to establish whether short-term and long-term memories are processed and encoded in different ways, and whether the sound and meaning of words influenced these types of memory store.

Baddeley split his participants into four groups and presented each with a slide show of ten words. To investigate the effect of sound and meaning on memory, each group was given a slightly different set of words which were either linked acoustically (and therefore sounded similar), linked semantically (so had similar meanings), or two control groups where the words were not acoustically or semantically similar. The four groups were:

- Acoustically similar words (e.g.; pen, pad, pan, pap)
- Acoustically dissimilar words (e.g.; hen, day, few)
- Semantically similar words (e.g.; small, tiny, little)
- Semantically dissimilar words (e.g.; hot, old, late)

<< CHAPTER 5

Psychologists have investigated in depth how memory functions.

After being presented with the words each group experienced an interference activity designed to prevent them from simply repeating the words in their head. This activity involved them listening to and then writing down eight numbers three times. They were then asked to recall the words they had been shown in the correct order. These procedures were repeated four times to test the participants' short-term memory, then a fifth and final trial was conducted to test long-term memory. In this trial the participants were asked to perform an interference task for 15 minutes and then try again to remember the correct order of the words they had been shown.

Baddeley found that acoustically similar words were harder to recall than acoustically dissimilar words, and semantically similar words were more difficult to recall than semantically dissimilar ones. Short-term recall tended to be more negatively affected by acoustic similarity, and long-term recall tended to be more negatively affected by semantic similarity.

This research gives us an insight into how an internal mental process, memory, works by manipulating the input a person is given and then measuring the output to infer what may be happening in the mind. The results suggest that our short-term memory relies more on sound and long-term memory relies more on meaning, which may explain why we feel the need to repeat out loud sequences of numbers, such as telephone numbers, when we are trying to remember them in the short term.

THE EFFECT OF LANGUAGE ON MEMORY

How input from our environment can affect an internal mental process was also demonstrated very effectively by Elizabeth Loftus and John Palmer in 1974. In their study 'Reconstruction of Automobile Destruction: An Example of the Interaction Between Language and Memory', they investigated how leading questions can influence memory in the form of eyewitness testimony of a car accident.

In their study 45 American students were shown seven short video clips of a vehicle collision. They were then split into five groups. Each group was asked the same question, but the verb used to describe the collision was altered for each group. One group was asked 'about how fast were the cars going when they smashed into each other?', and for the other groups the verb 'smashed' was replaced with 'collided', 'bumped', 'hit', or 'contacted'. They found that the verb used influenced the participants' estimate of the speed of the vehicles as follows:

VERB USED	MEAN SPEED ESTIMATE (MPH)
Smashed	40.8
Collided	39.3
Bumped	38.1
Hit	34.0
Contacted	31.8

They also conducted a second experiment to investigate the longer-term effects of leading questions on our memory. One hundred and fifty participants were shown a short clip of a multi-vehicle accident and asked questions about what they had seen. The participants were split into three groups and one question was changed for each group. One group was asked 'how fast were the cars going when they hit each other?', another was asked 'how fast were the cars going when they smashed into each other?', and a third control group was not asked this question at all. One week later all participants were asked ten questions about the accident, including a critical question 'did you see any broken glass?'. There was no broken glass shown in the clip. Loftus and Palmer found that in all three conditions the majority of participants correctly responded that they did not see any broken glass, but in the 'smashed' verb condition more than double the number of participants recalled seeing glass compared to the other two groups.

	VERB CONDITION		
Response	Smashed	Hit	Control
Yes	16	7	6
No	34	43	44

COGNITIVE PSYCHOLOGY >>

This research is another good example of how we can study internal mental processes by manipulating the input a person receives and then studying the effect this has on the output. In this case, we can see that the cognitive process of memory can be influenced by information provided after the event. Memory is not merely a record of what we experience at the time, but is a dynamic process which can be influenced by factors such as leading questions. Research such as this has important implications for any situation where accurate recall of an event is essential, such as crime witness testimony. The cognitive interview technique now used by police specifically aims to avoid the use of leading questions and therefore enhance the accuracy of witness recall.

Loftus and Palmer found that using the words 'hit' and 'smash' triggered very different responses from their subjects.

PIAGET AND COGNITIVE DEVELOPMENT

Swiss psychologist Jean Piaget was the first to introduce the concept of schemas as a way to understand the world around us. Piaget was interested in child cognitive development and the education of children. He popularized the idea of the 'child as scientist', suggesting that children learn by performing experiments, making observations, and learning from these experiences. Part of this experimenting included the development of schemas.

Piaget suggested that as we develop we acquire small packets of information called schemas that help us to understand the world around us. When we are exposed to a new experience or piece of information we add this to our bank of schemas, a process he called assimilation. We may also need to modify our existing schemas or create new ones based on this new information, a process known as 'accommodation'. In this way schemas are continually adapted and refined. We have schemas relating to tangible objects such as animals or vehicles. For example, when a child first learns a schema to use the word 'car' to label an object with wheels then they may begin by calling all vehicles 'car', whether it is a car, lorry or tractor. Eventually a more experienced person will tell the child that the object they see is actually a tractor. The child may then pay attention to the features that separate the car from the tractor – maybe larger back wheels – assimilate this new information, and accommodate this information by creating a new schema for a tractor. We also have schemas for non-tangible things such as behaviours in given situations; for example, our schema for which behaviours are acceptable in a classroom or a theatre will be different to our schema of acceptable behaviours at a party or a theme park.

Piaget also believed that humans experience four stages of cognitive development as they interact with the world and gain knowledge. He believed that all humans pass through these stages in a set order, but they may do so at different ages depending on factors such as their biological maturity, their experiences in life, and the support they receive when interacting with their environment.

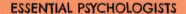
ESSENTIAL PSYCHOLOGISTS

Jean Piaget
Lived: 1896–1980
Origin: Switzerland
Known for: Stages of Cognitive Development

COGNITIVE PSYCHOLOGY >> 71

Stage	Age	Description	Example behaviours
Sensorimotor	0–2	Children learn by interacting with their environment. Predominantly relies on senses and motor functions.	Children develop an understanding of cause and effect, for example bashing a hard object on the floor makes a noise; and object permanence, which is the ability to realize an object continues to exist once they can no longer see it.
Pre-operational	2–7	Children begin to understand symbols, symbolic play and language. They are still egocentric and tend only to be able to see the world and situations from their own perspective.	Children begin to engage in pretend or imaginative play, and may reference events that have happened in the past or people who are not in the room.
Concrete operational	7–11	Children develop a stronger understanding of cause and effect relationships and begin to be more logical in their thinking, so long as the concept is concrete and observable.	Children understand the principle of conservation, which is that objects can change shape or arrangement but still have the same volume, value or number.
Formal operational	12+	Children develop abstract thinking and can construct hypotheses for novel scenarios that they have not yet experienced. They develop the ability to be able to consider moral or ethical issues from the point of view of others.	Children at this stage can use what is known as 'hypothetical-deductive reasoning', meaning that they can apply reasoning in a systematic way to answer a question.

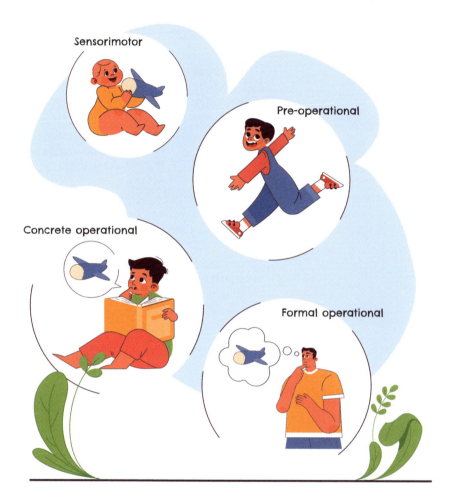

Stages of cognitive development.

The cognitive approach uses scientific methods that are measurable and repeatable in order to build a picture of what may be happening in the 'black box' that is the human mind. Studies such as those mentioned in this chapter provide objective data that can be analysed, replicated and built upon to help us both understand and predict how internal mental processes function. However, it can be argued that many studies in this area do not replicate the conditions of real life. For example, the participants watching the videos of car accidents in Loftus and Palmer's study may not have felt the intense emotions that are experienced when witnessing an accident in real life. Furthermore, by using the scientific method to study psychology, approaches such as the cognitive approach have to reduce their focus down to testable and measurable variables, focusing as much as possible on the one specific area of interest they are aiming to study. This means that they can be accused of being reductionist, meaning they reduce human experience to a single factor and ignore others, such as the biological explanations for the workings of our memory. However, not all approaches in psychology take this reductionist approach, one notable example being the humanistic approach which is the subject of our next chapter.

Cognitive Psychology in Everyday Life: Cognitive Behavioural Therapy (CBT)

CBT works on the premise that it is the way that we perceive a situation, rather than the situation itself, that can lead to poor mental health and unhappiness. It aims to alter dysfunctional or unhelpful perceptions by changing these perceptions and altering our cognition. Some basic methods used during CBT and how they link to cognitive psychology include:

- Keeping a dysfunctional thought diary which is used to identify faulty internal mental processing. This strategy encourages the patient to identify situations or triggers to their dysfunctional thoughts (inputs), reflect on their thoughts or feelings in reaction to these triggers (processes), then analyse their behaviour or reaction to the trigger (outputs).
- Cognitive restructuring to alter faulty mental processes. This strategy aims to alter schemas that a patient may have developed in relation to a situation or trigger. The therapist will support the patient to replace irrational thoughts and schemas with more rational ones. For example, if an irrational thought is identified as being when a friend ignores your text message they must no longer like you; a more rational thought may be that they were just busy that day or have forgotten to reply.
- Pleasant activity-scheduling to encourage healthy internal mental processes. This strategy intends to improve a patient's self-schemas and self-concept by encouraging them to take part in activities that encourage positive thoughts and a sense of happiness or achievement.

Cognitive behavioural therapy.

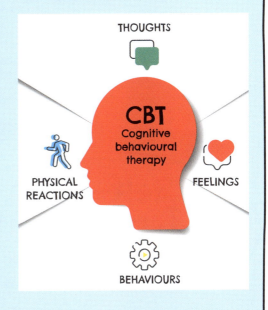

Chapter 6
Humanistic Approach

- Hierarchy of Needs
- Person-Centred Therapy
- Self-Actualization
- Congruence

HUMANISTIC APPROACH >>

UNLIKE MANY OF THE OTHER APPROACHES discussed so far which attempt to provide universal rules or theories to explain human behaviour, the humanistic approach emphasizes the importance of considering each person as a unique individual. It aims to consider the whole person and their motivations.

Humanistic psychology rejected the deterministic viewpoints of the psychodynamic and behaviourist approaches which both suggest that our behaviour is largely determined by factors outside of our control. It emphasized instead the concept of free will. Unlike the behaviourist approach, it assumes that human psychology is unique and therefore can only be understood by studying humans, not other animals.

ASSUMPTIONS

The humanistic approach is optimistic about human nature and assumes that humans are inherently good. It acknowledges that humans have free will and personal agency, and are driven by individual, personal goals to achieve their potential. Their circumstances and previous experiences do not determine or constrain their behaviour, and people have agency and an ability to self-actualize.

It also assumes that individuals should be studied and their personal environmental context and drives should be considered, rather than conducting large-scale studies which aim to identify the behaviour of the average person, or generate theories based on statistical analysis of large groups. A psychologist working from a humanistic perspective would use what are called qualitative methods which don't necessarily generate statistical data. These methods include strategies such as case studies of individuals using informal interviews or content analysis of speech or behaviour.

MASLOW'S HIERARCHY OF NEEDS

Abraham Maslow (1908–70) was a pioneering theorist in humanistic psychology. He was born in Brooklyn, New York to Jewish immigrants from Russia and was the eldest of seven children. He would later describe his childhood as lonely and would spend much of his childhood in

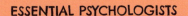

ESSENTIAL PSYCHOLOGISTS

Abraham Maslow
Lived: 1908–1970
Origin: United States of America
Known for: Hierarchy of Needs

KEY VOCABULARY

Deterministic	The idea that all human behaviours result from previous events in a person's life.
Psychodynamic approach	The relationship between the unconscious and conscious parts of the mind and emotional forces that determine personality and motivation.
Behaviourist approach	The idea that all behaviours are learned exclusively through interaction with the environment.
Self-actualize	A person's desire to realize their full potential.
Qualitative	Measuring the quality of something rather than the quantity.
Empirical	Using observable and quantifiable data to research psychological phenomena.
Psychotherapy	A general term to describe the method of treating psychological disorders through talking therapy and psychological techniques.
Incongruence	A mismatch between one's perceived ideal self and actual self, leading to an imbalance in personality and emotional distress.
Humanistic psychology	An approach in psychology that studies the whole person and emphasizes free will, and an individual's potential for self-actualization.

HUMANISTIC APPROACH >>

libraries, finding comfort in reading books. Maslow originally began studying law but then switched to study psychology at the University of Wisconsin. It was here that his interest in psychology was influenced by his mentor Harry Harlow and his research into attachment in Rhesus monkeys. In 1934 he earned his doctoral degree and in 1937 began his academic career at Brooklyn College.

Throughout this period Maslow attempted to construct a theory that explained human needs and motivation. He based his studies on people identified as being self-actualizing personalities and which he viewed as the supreme achievers in society. This included politicians and scientists such as Abraham Lincoln, Albert Einstein, Eleanor Roosevelt and many others. He analysed the characteristics and personality traits they possessed that allowed them to be healthy, creative and successful individuals. Maslow discovered that they shared similar traits such as being creative, loving, compassionate,

Maslow's hierarchy of needs

Physiological needs: Essential for survival, these are the most fundamental human needs, such as air, water, food, shelter, clothing and sleep. Maslow argued that these basic needs must be met before individuals can transition to the next stage of the hierarchy.

Safety needs: After physiological needs are fulfilled, needs such as health and wellbeing, personal safety, financial security, and resilience to accidents and illness become important.

Love and belongingness needs: Social needs then emerge once physiological and safety needs have been met. Maslow highlighted the importance of love, affection and belonging for human wellbeing. This has its foundation in family and social groups but can also be found through emotional relationships such as friendships and romantic attachments.

Esteem needs: These needs can be separated into two groups: esteem for oneself (dignity, achievement, mastery, independence) and the desire for admiration and respect from others (status, prestige). Satisfying these needs results in feelings of self-worth and confidence.

Self-actualization needs: These needs are found at the highest level of the hierarchy. Self-actualization refers to self-fulfilment, pursuing personal growth, and the realization of an individual's potential. Maslow described self-actualization as the desire to become everything one is capable of becoming.

empathetic, spontaneous and open-minded. Crucially the majority of self-actualizers had a firm awareness of reality, recognizing what they could not influence while at the same time confronting problems that they were able to control and resolve. From this they would experience intense 'peak experiences' that would give them a feeling of meaningfulness that they would then repeatedly seek out. They also shared a strong sense of belonging and maintained healthy relationships within small social groups. Maslow described people who are self-actualized as displaying a 'coherent personality syndrome' representing optimal psychological wellbeing.

In 1943 he introduced his 'hierarchy of needs' in a paper titled 'A Theory of Human Motivation' and later expanded on his original work in his 1954 book *Motivation and Personality*. He proposed that human beings have certain fundamental needs and that these are organized in a hierarchy. The hierarchy is typically depicted as a pyramid with the most fundamental needs required for survival at the base and the highest level needs at the top, with self-actualization forming the peak of the pyramid.

Maslow stressed that it was essential to fulfil each underlying need before an individual could move up the hierarchy towards the higher level needs. He would later emphasize that it was not essential for a person to necessarily satisfy all of the requirements of each stage in order for them to progress and recognized that this process continued throughout a person's lifetime. Maslow also described how the pyramid could be applied to a specific area of a person's life cycle such as their motivation to become a good parent.

However, for some individuals, progress through the hierarchy can be disrupted either due to a failure to meet the needs of the underlying stage or through external factors. These could be life events such as chronic illness, loss of income or homelessness. Therefore, despite a person having a desire to progress through the different stages, their course may fluctuate throughout their life and they may move back and forward through the hierarchy.

Maslow's hierarchy has been criticized for lacking empirical evidence and for reflecting Western values and ideologies. Therefore self-actualization may take a different course in other cultures and its holistic approach means there is likely to be a great deal of variation across individuals. There is no absolute formula to achieve self-actualization. However, Maslow was one of the first to study psychologically healthy individuals which was a leap forward in the humanistic approach. His hierarchy of needs has seen useful applications in education, supporting pupils from disadvantaged backgrounds and has been a key tool in enabling social mobility.

HUMANISTIC APPROACH >>

Maslow's approach is perhaps best summed up in his own words: 'It is as if Freud supplied us the sick half of psychology and we must now fill it out with the healthy half.'

CARL ROGERS AND THE PERSON-CENTRED APPROACH

Carl Rogers was a pioneering figure in the development of humanistic psychology. Rogers was a prominent psychologist and is best known for developing a person-centred approach to therapy. He significantly advanced our understanding of the self and personality and like Maslow, Rogers embraced free will and self-determination. His work focused on the

Humanistic psychology emphasizes the unique nature of the human mind.

ESSENTIAL PSYCHOLOGISTS

Carl Rogers
Lived: 1902–1987
Origin: United States of America
Known for: Person-Centred Therapy

importance of the therapeutic relationship and the growth potential of healthy individuals as well as self-actualization. Rogers described this as our basic motive to realize our full potential, devising the term 'actualizing tendency'.

Rogers' most significant contribution was developing what he termed the client-centred therapy which later became more commonly referred to as person-centred therapy. Rogers believed that people were inherently good and that given the right environmental conditions they would flourish and reach their potential. His methods centred on removing obstacles, freeing the patient to grow and develop in a normal way. They were also non-directive, meaning that the therapist facilitated the patient to lead the conversation between themselves and the therapist. This assisted people in taking responsibility for themselves rather than being guided by the therapist.

Rogers recorded his therapeutic sessions and analysed the transcripts. He was the first to publish complete cases of psychotherapy and from this research he developed three core concepts towards his therapeutic sessions: unconditional positive regard, empathy and genuineness.

Rogers was the first to take this approach to viewing oneself in an unconditional, positive way that avoided unduly harsh judgement of the self. He argued that this acceptance was crucial for the patient's self-development, creating an environment where patients felt safe and understood. He also stressed the importance of empathy and the therapist's ability to understand the perspective of the patient and validate their feelings. Rogers emphasized that the therapist should be genuine (also known as 'congruence') and transparent in order to build a trusting and open relationship with the patient in order to guide them to wellness. Using these techniques and giving control to the patient was a leap forward and revolutionized the field of humanistic psychology.

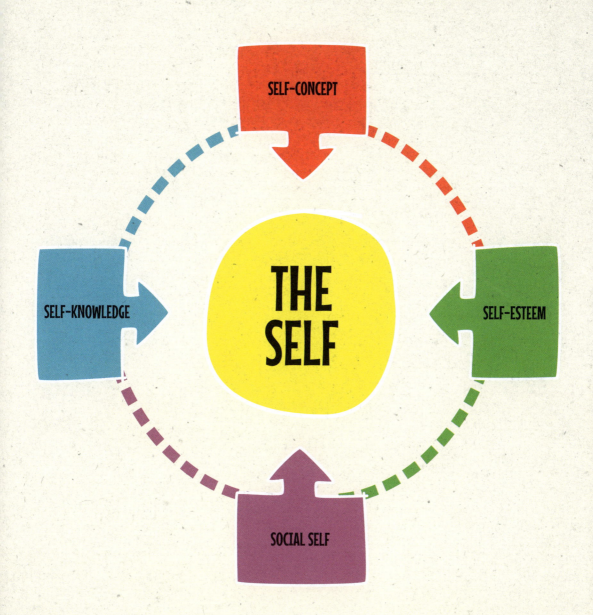

Rogers' idea of self-concept.

IDEAL SELF VERSUS THE REAL SELF

Central to Rogers' theory is the notion of self-concept which he defined as an organized set of perceptions and beliefs held by an individual about themselves. In order for a person to achieve self-actualization they must have consistency between one's 'ideal self' and the 'real self'. The real self is the person you actually are and the ideal self is the person you aspire to be. Rogers believed that a healthy self-concept is fundamental to personal growth. Congruence is when we experience similar perceptions about our ideal self and our real self. When our sense of self is accurate this is known as 'high congruence' and is characterized by a greater sense of self-worth and a healthy, productive life. However, if there is a large discrepancy between the two perceptions of the real self and ideal self this can lead to a state of psychological distress. Rogers termed this 'incongruence' and saw that it could sometimes lead to individuals not being able to cope with the demands of everyday life. The goal of Rogers' approach to therapy was to bring the real self and the ideal self into alignment so that the patient could build their self-esteem, self-actualize and fulfil their true potential.

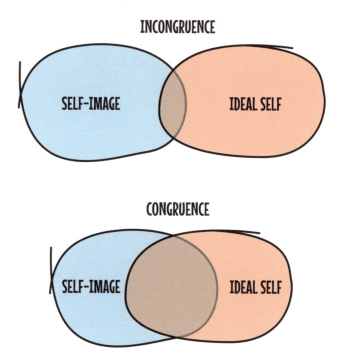

Congruence and incongruence.

THE GOOD LIFE

We know that happiness doesn't just come to people and that there are things we can do to actively increase our happiness. Maslow saw that there were external factors that existed in a hierarchical organization that affected an individual's quality of life. Rogers' assumption was that a fully functioning person will continually aim to fulfil their potential. Rather than moving through static stages towards an end goal, Rogers viewed the principles of the 'good life' as operating in a fluid way that was a continuous and changing process. In this sense Rogers defined the good life as a process rather than a state of being: 'It is a direction not a destination' (Carl Rogers, 1967). It is important to remember that Rogers saw the fully functioning person as an ideal and one that people ultimately won't achieve. However, he identified five character traits of the fully functioning person:

1. Openness to experience: Where both positive and negative emotions are accepted. There is a move away from ego defensiveness and problems are worked through.
2. Existential lifestyle: Being able to completely appreciate the present and events as they occur in the moment, rarely looking back to the past or forward to the future.
3. Trust feelings: We trust ourselves to make the right decisions, paying attention to our gut feelings and instincts. People's own decisions are the right ones and they make the right choices.
4. Creativity: Creative thinking, risk-taking and seeking new experiences are integral to the person's life. They do not feel a need to conform.
5. A rich, full life: Seeking out new experiences and challenges, leading to the person being happy and satisfied with life.

Carl Rogers' work had a profound impact on psychology and the understanding of personality development. The person-centred approach he developed has been integrated into many areas of counselling and psychotherapy. His work was also influential in establishing the guidance and procedures associated with therapeutic psychology, introducing important concepts around consent and patient confidentiality. While critics argue that there is little empirical data to support Rogers' approach and that the ideal person represents a Western construct it was a leap forward to look at healthy individuals rather than just those in need of psychological intervention. In this regard Carl Rogers broadened the appeal of psychology and understanding of how to improve our psychological wellbeing and live 'the good life'.

Chapter 7

Positive Psychology

Positive Approach

The Good Life

Aversive Conditioning

Treating Depression

Learned Helplessness

POSITIVE PSYCHOLOGY

The positive approach in psychology emerged towards the end of the 20th century. American psychologist Martin Seligman pioneered the approach, which focuses primarily on the positive aspects of human nature, the 'good' qualities that people possess, and how they can be nurtured.

Positive psychology emerged at a time when many researchers began to believe that psychology had been dominated by a focus on the negative aspects of the human experience. Much research had been conducted on psychological pathology, on investigating and treating the negative aspects of psychology such as stress and mental illness. There was little focus on how to enhance the human experience. It was proposed that a 'shift' was needed in order to understand how people could flourish as individuals.

As a result, positive psychology focuses on the belief that people wish to enhance their lives, to make their lives more meaningful, and to increase their levels of happiness in order to achieve greater fulfilment.

As Seligman remarked: 'Psychology should be just as concerned with building strength as with repairing damage.'

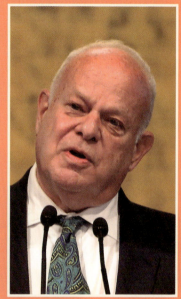

ESSENTIAL PSYCHOLOGISTS

Martin Seligman
Lived: 1942–
Origin: United States of America
Known for: Positive Psychology

ASSUMPTIONS

Unlike other approaches in psychology that have been criticized for their deterministic view of human behaviour (see Chapter 10, Debates in Psychology), the positive approach acknowledges the concept of free will. It argues that our actions are a result of our own choice and agency, and are not pre-determined by external factors.

The positive approach also proposes that positive human traits are every bit as authentic and worthy of study as negative traits. It aims to celebrate the good things in life. Therapies that are linked to the positive approach focus on strategies to enable wellbeing and happiness, rather than on 'fixing' mental ill health. The positive approach suggests that we are happiest when we are able to utilize traits known as our signature strengths. Signature strengths are features of our character that are most essential to who we are or who we perceive ourselves to be. These may be traits such as a love of learning, humour, creativity or kindness.

Positive psychology has links to ideas suggested by Carl Rogers in our chapter on humanism, as it also suggests a concept known as 'the good life'. This refers to factors that contribute to what we might consider a well-lived life. Seligman proposed three aspects that contribute to the good life:

- The pleasant life – happiness comes from pursuing positive emotions in relation to the past, present and future. For example, focusing on positive memories in relation to ourselves and others, rather than negative ones.
- The good life – happiness comes from pursuing activities that positively absorb and engage us. For example, making time to pursue a craft or sport that gives us a feeling of positive achievement.
- The meaningful life – happiness comes from a deep sense of fulfilment by living for a purpose much greater than oneself. For example, using your strengths and skills positively by volunteering for a charity or caring for another person.

Seligman also suggested that the good life is the combination of three elements:

- Positive connection to others – being able to trust others, express love, forgive mistakes and enjoy being happy with others.
- Positive individual traits – recognizing personal qualities that we feel positively about, such as a sense of integrity, creativity, bravery, and so on.
- Life regulation qualities – these are qualities that enable us to self-regulate and manage our behaviour to achieve our goals. For example, feeling a sense of autonomy and independence, and having faith in our own ability to make decisions.

KEY VOCABULARY	
Collectivist culture	These cultures stress the importance of cooperation and prioritize the needs of the group over the needs of the individual. For example, China and Ghana.
Individualistic culture	These cultures stress the needs of the individual over the needs of the group or society. They would prioritize individuality, independence and personal achievement. For example, North America and western Europe.

POSITIVE PSYCHOLOGY >>

WELLBEING ≠ HAPPINESS

WELLBEING

POSITIVE EMOTION

ENGAGEMENT

RELATIONSHIPS

MEANING

ACCOMPLISHMENT

SELIGMAN AND POSITIVE PSYCHOLOGY

For much of his career he investigated a concept that came to be known as 'learned helplessness', a passive response we have when faced by problems we cannot solve or control.

Throughout the 1960s a series of classic experiments using dogs was conducted by Seligman and Steven Maier investigating a phenomenon identified by Ivan Pavlov known as 'aversive conditioning' or 'avoidance learning'. The animals placed in a crate would receive electric shocks from the floor, which were preceded by a stimulus such as a tone or a flashing light. The idea was that the dogs would connect the stimuli with the impending shock and learn to avoid it by jumping over a barrier. However, Seligman wanted to see if the association that some of the dogs had learned could be reversed by placing the dogs in a position where they could not escape the shock.

In one experiment, the dogs were placed in a rubberized harness that allowed their legs to hang down so that an electric shock could be administered to their hind legs. The dog's head was placed between two plates and by pressing the plates the dog could stop the shock from occurring. However, some of the dogs were placed in a harness where the plates had been rigged so that they did not stop the shock. Even if the dogs pressed the plates the electric shock would continue for some 30 seconds and would continue repeating despite the number of times the dogs pressed the plates with their head.

Both groups of dogs were then returned to the shuttle box with an electrified grid on one side separated by a barrier with the non-electric floor on the other. This time both sets of dogs had the opportunity to end their pain easily and quickly by jumping over the barrier. What they found was that the group of dogs that had the functional head panels quickly learned to jump the barrier, whereas the dogs with the non-functional barriers didn't even try to escape the shock. After a week of trials several of the dogs remained unwilling or unable to jump the barrier to avoid the shock. The effects of these experiments had severe implications and a legacy that Seligman could not have predicted. What they appeared to have observed was 'learned helplessness' which is a learned response where an individual feels they have no control over what happens to them. It can be characterized by:

- Lack of motivation. When faced with a new or difficult situation, failing to respond or giving up before you even try to solve a problem.
- Emotional withdrawal. People can be emotionally flat or withdrawn in response to stressful or painful situations.

POSITIVE PSYCHOLOGY >>

Positive psychology focuses on the good aspects of human nature.

- Barriers to success. People who experience learned helplessness may have difficulty in learning from success and applying their success to future situations.

Seligman wanted to understand if the effect could be reversed in the dogs but did not want to cause the dogs any further harm unless the experiments had value in bettering people's lives. He realized that his research with the dogs could have profound impacts for the way mental disorders such as depression could be viewed.

Seligman and Maier set out to find a way to reverse the effect of learned helplessness. They found that by making one small adjustment to the process they could effectively reverse the effect in the dogs. By trialling

Seligman and Maier's learned helplessness experiment.

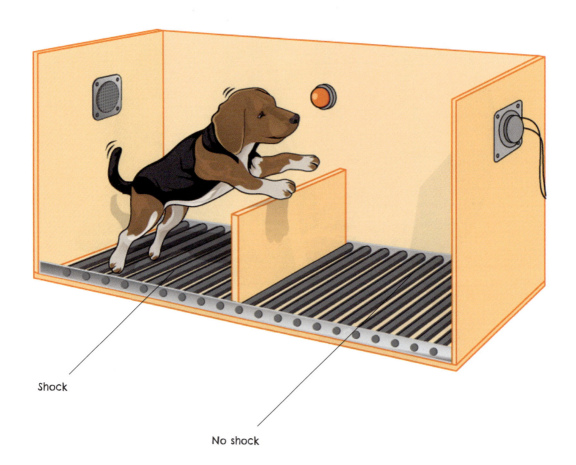

Shock

No shock

the shuttle box experiment before the dogs were placed in the harness they had managed to learn that they could control the electric shock. Even when the dogs received repeated shocks in the harness they didn't give up. Seligman realized if the effect could be reversed in dogs then there was the possibility that learned helplessness could therefore be reversed in humans and mental disorders such as depression could be treated effectively.

Over the following decades Seligman worked to apply the findings of the studies with dogs to humans, developing cognitive behavioural therapies to treat depression. He also conducted longitudinal studies following the impacts of early intervention programmes with children which helped them to overcome learned helplessness from a young age. In 1995 Seligman and his colleagues published their results. These showed positive impacts with the schoolchildren in the test group. They developed significantly lower rates of depression when compared to the control group and the risk factors associated with developing depression reduced after treatment.

Then in 2014 the story of Martin Seligman's research took a sinister turn. The US Senate Intelligence Committee released a report containing hundreds of pages detailing the interrogation and torture of terror suspects following the 9/11 attacks. Some of the most brutal techniques had been developed by two psychologists, James E. Mitchell and Bruce Jessen. They had no background in intelligence or interrogation. Instead they had developed an experimental programme of psychological torture based on the theories of learned helplessness. They created a situation that was deemed uncontrollable by the captive and reasoned that this would induce a state of depression in the detainee who would then cooperate with the interrogators. When Seligman learned of the report he was shocked and said that he 'grieved for the good science which has helped many people overcome depression.' What is even more astounding is that Seligman had met one of the Central Intelligence Agency (CIA) psychologists at a private function just months before the programme of interrogation was initiated. The CIA believed that using learned helplessness would result in the captives telling the truth. However, the evidence suggests that people subjected to this treatment would tell the interrogator what they wanted to hear rather than telling the truth to end the discomfort and gain back control. In fact it also may have the opposite effect in reinforcing that telling the truth results in no change in conditions. Learned helplessness is therefore an unreliable interrogation method but a very effective torture method leaving long-lasting effects.

Key Research: Myers and Diener (1995)

American psychologists David Myers and Ed Diener conducted what is known as a literature review of previous research into aspects of positive psychology. Their publication, titled 'Who is Happy?', reviewed a range of research, including correlational studies, observations and questionnaires regarding subjective wellbeing. They suggested that their research would be a welcome complement to the many studies into depression and anxiety, helping people to rethink their priorities and enhance their wellbeing.

Myers and Diener presented their findings under the following headings:

Myths of happiness

Myers and Diener found that age, gender and race had little impact on happiness. For example, in a survey they reviewed around 170,000 people from 16 different countries, and discovered that no one age group reported being significantly happier than another (Inglehart, 1990).

They did find, however, that different cultures showed significant differences in how they reported happiness. The same survey mentioned above found that around 10 per cent of people in Portugal reported being very happy compared to 40 per cent of people in the Netherlands. However, the cause of this difference is unclear. The researchers noted that collectivist cultures reported lower subjective wellbeing than individualist cultures, and suggested this difference could be due to the greater emphasis on the importance of individual experience of, and expression of happiness in these cultures.

Happy people

The researchers found that those people who reported greatest happiness shared certain similarities. They mention that in one National Institute on Aging study, the happiest people in 1973 were still reporting happiness a decade later, despite changes in their lives that may have negatively

affected their outlook such as changes in their work, home and family (Costa, McCrae, & Zonderman, 1987). The researchers asked themselves 'Who are these chronically happy people?'

- Traits: Happy people shared similar traits such as high self-esteem and a sense of personal control. They agreed with statements such as 'I am a lot of fun to be with'.
- Relationships: People who could name several friends with whom they could share their intimate concerns reported greater happiness. They were also healthier and less likely to die prematurely.
- The flow of happy people: People with higher work satisfaction also reported better life satisfaction. The researchers suggested that work provides a sense of personal identity: it also adds to a sense of community and supports the previous point regarding relationships, in that work can offer people a network of relationships. Work can also offer a sense of purpose.
- The faith of happy people: The research reviewed by Myers and Diener suggested that religious people are much less likely to become delinquent, abuse drugs or commit suicide. Religious people reported higher happiness and life satisfaction. The researchers suggested several possible reasons for this link. Perhaps religion provided supportive relationships, a sense of purpose, or hope when presented with difficult situations.

What is unclear from this review is whether these similarities caused happiness and a sense of subjective wellbeing in the participants, or if being inherently a happier and more positive person brought about these similarities. For example, having strong friendships and good work flow was correlated with greater happiness, but could it be argued that people with a positive outlook are more likely to have a larger friendship group and find work more easily?

POSITIVE PSYCHOLOGY >>

Chapter 8
Biological Theory

- Adaptationism
- Localization of Function
- Neurotransmission
- Brain Imaging

BIOLOGICAL THEORY >>   95

The biological approach to psychology has made great strides in recent years due to the advent of new technologies. Modern biological psychology draws on our knowledge of areas such as evolution, brain structure and neurotransmission to study and explain behaviour, as well as advanced brain imaging technology.

The use of biological knowledge and theory in an attempt to understand human behaviour is not new. For example, Freud believed that much of our behaviour is driven by our biology in the form of innate biological drives, suggesting the id as a component of our personality that drives our behaviour in response to instinctual, biological urges, seeking only gratification through physically pleasurable experience such as eating or having sex.

Surgeries that aimed to alter the brain in order to influence human behaviour have been performed since prehistoric times in the form of trepanation, which is the drilling of a hole in the head. It is believed this was performed to relieve pain or possibly to treat mental illness by pulling spirits from the body. More modern psychosurgery is believed to have first been performed in 1888 when Swiss psychologist Gottlieb Burckhardt removed the brain areas of six patients that he believed were associated with aggression and hallucinations.

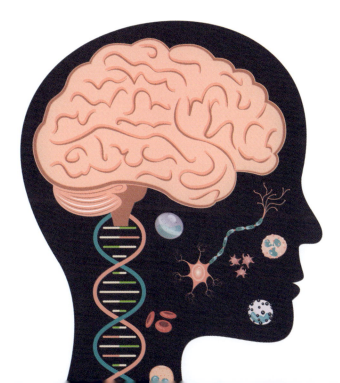

Biological psychology seeks to understand the structure of the brain and nervous system to explain human behaviour.

ESSENTIAL PSYCHOLOGISTS

John Bowlby
Lived: 1907–1990
Origin: United Kingdom
Known for: Environment of Evolutionary Adaptiveness

ASSUMPTIONS

The biological approach to psychology assumes that our understanding of evolution and what is known as our 'environment of evolutionary adaptiveness' can be used to explain certain behaviours. It assumes that we may be able to explain some human behaviours by understanding the conditions and evolutionary pressures our species was under while it evolved to exist in its current state. This is known as an 'adaptationist approach'.

This approach also assumes that different areas of the brain perform different and specific functions. This is known as 'localization of function'. Techniques used in this area of research range from studying patients who have experienced damage or trauma to certain areas of the brain, to using technology such as computerized tomography (CT) to view structures in the brain, or functional magnetic resonance imaging (fMRI) which enables us to study the brain as it is working.

Our knowledge of neurotransmission and the chemical neurotransmitters that carry impulses in our brains has helped us to identify neurotransmitters that are associated with specific behaviours or moods. This has also enabled us to alter and treat behaviours with drugs that in turn alter how these neurotransmitters work.

ADAPTATIONISM AND THE ENVIRONMENT OF EVOLUTIONARY ADAPTIVENESS

Psychologist John Bowlby first introduced the concept of the 'environment of evolutionary adaptiveness' (EEA) in 1969. It does not refer to a specific place, but rather a set of circumstances and pressures under which a species has evolved to exist in its current state, and that these pressures do not just influence the physical evolution of a species but also influence the behaviours of that species. Bowlby proposed that the behaviour of a species will be most efficient in this environment, and that there is a mismatch between our modern way of living and our EEA. He believed that this mismatch can be used to explain some common behaviours which seem maladaptive in our current world but may have been useful traits for our ancestors.

This concept of behavioural evolution can be used to explain some common phobias, for example phobias of snakes or spiders. People who live in areas that contain few, or even no, dangerous snakes or spiders still commonly have a fear of these creatures. It could be argued that in our EEA there were snakes and spiders that were dangerous and could potentially kill us with one bite. People who were predisposed to avoid these animals were less likely to get bitten and die. They will therefore survive longer, be more likely to reproduce, and pass those genes on to their offspring. So it is not only physical but also behavioural characteristics that may be altered through evolution.

Another example is that in our EEA humans would most likely have lived in small communities of around 30 to 50 individuals. We may have developed psychological mechanisms to ensure that we integrate into our small community and ensure its success, but have little reason to be invested in the success of other communities of strangers. This conflicts with our modern world in which we are directly and indirectly connected with vast communities of people who are strangers to us. Through technology and global trade our behaviours and decisions affect people and communities far beyond our immediate social group, and as a species we are poorly equipped to manage global social dilemmas.

KEY VOCABULARY	
Innate	Traits existing in an animal or person from birth, rather than those that can be learned, essential to nature or character.
Neuron	A single nerve cell transmitting and receiving electrochemical messages.
Neurotransmitter/ Neurotransmission	Chemical messengers or molecules such as serotonin and dopamine that carry, enhance and balance signals between neurons and target cells throughout the body.
Cerebral cortex	The cerebral cortex is the folded outer grey layer of the brain made up from tightly packed neurons. It is associated with various complex cognitive processes and higher-level functions including thought, memory, perception, attention, language, consciousness and advanced motor functions.
Dendrite	A branch-like projection of a neuron that receives information from other neurons.
Enzyme	Molecules, generally proteins, which speed up the rate of bio-chemical reactions without itself becoming altered.

LOCALIZATION OF FUNCTION IN THE BRAIN

Most of us are familiar with an image of the brain as a grey, jelly-like blob covered in swirling crevices, but the brain is in fact formed from many different layers and structures. Functions of the brain are thought to be coordinated by different structures or locations in the brain, hence the term localization of function.

The outer layer of the brain, known as the cerebral cortex, is only a few millimetres thick but owing to its many folds (known as sulci and gyri) it actually has a large surface area and accounts for around half the mass of the brain. The cerebral cortex makes up a larger structure known as the cerebrum, which itself is divided into several lobes, each associated with different functions.

- Frontal lobe: thinking, speaking, memory, movement.
- Temporal lobe: hearing, learning, emotions, fear.
- Parietal lobe: language, touch, taste, smell.
- Occipital lobe: vision, colours, letters, orientation.

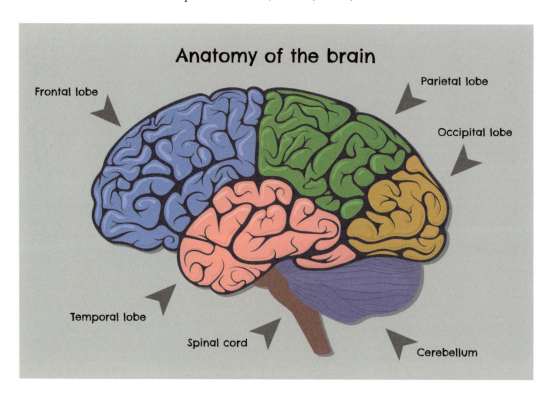

BIOLOGICAL THEORY >>

The areas known as subcortical structures include the hypothalamus and pituitary gland which are associated with the production of hormones, the limbic systems which are associated with memory and emotions such as fear, and the basal ganglia which are associated with motor functions and movement.

The brain stem is where the brain forms a connection with the rest of our nervous system through the medulla oblongata, which is connected to our spinal cord. The medulla oblongata regulates basic essential functions like heart rate and breathing. The brain stem also contains an area known as the pons which contains nuclei associated with functions such as touch and pain. At the back of the brain between the medulla and the brain stem is the cerebellum, which looks like a large blob and is associated with voluntary movement and coordination.

The brain is also divided into two hemispheres, left and right, which are connected by a thick bundle of nerve tissue known as the corpus callosum. The corpus callosum allows each hemisphere of the brain to communicate and coordinate functions. For example, the left hemisphere of the brain is largely responsible for language; however, the right hemisphere still plays a role in the processing of language, such as interpreting the emotional tone of speech.

The brain is divided into two distinct hemispheres.

Early evidence for localization of function in the brain comes from French neurosurgeon Paul Broca. In 1861 he studied patients who had difficulty producing language. He examined their brains after death and found that they had damage to an area of their left hemispheres, specifically the posterior portion of the frontal lobe. This has been named 'Broca's area' and is associated with speech production. Similarly, in 1874 Carl Wernicke, a German neurologist, discovered another area of the brain that was involved in language. His patients could speak and produce language, but were unable to understand language spoken to them. When he studied their brains he found lesions at a junction of the parietal, temporal and occipital lobes. This is now known as 'Wernicke's area'.

NEUROTRANSMISSION

Neurons are cells which transmit signals around our bodies in the form of electrical impulses. Neurons carry signals from receptor cells all over our bodies to our central nervous system, formed of the brain and spinal cord. These signals are called impulses and are passed on incredibly quickly at speeds of around 119 metres (390 feet) per second, and most of them we are completely unaware of. They control reflex actions such as our pupils contracting or dilating in response to light, or our pancreas releasing insulin into our blood to control our blood sugar levels. They also carry the signals that allow the brain to function and give us the cognition that enables us to think and feel.

Neurons have special adaptations to allow them to do their job. The cell body of a neuron is very long, and at each end it has many branches called axon terminals and dendrites, which allow them to connect to many other neurons in an intricate web of connectivity. However, at these branches the neurons do not physically connect to one another, but have a gap known as a synaptic cleft. Impulses are carried across this gap by chemicals known as neurotransmitters, and it is these neurotransmitters that we associate with specific behaviours and emotions. For example, low levels of serotonin have been associated with depression. However, it is not as simple as associating a specific neurotransmitter with a specific emotion. For example, the release of dopamine in the brain is linked to feelings of pleasure and satisfaction, but high levels of dopamine are also associated with some symptoms of schizophrenia such as hallucinations.

Our knowledge of neurotransmitters allows us to create drug therapies that alter the levels of certain neurotransmitters in the brain. For example, some

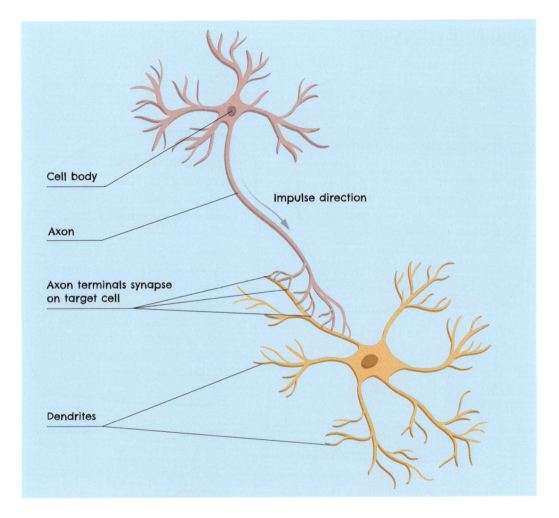

Anatomy of a neuron.

antipsychotic drugs work in the brain by blocking, but not stimulating, the receptor site on a neuron for dopamine and therefore reducing some of the symptoms of schizophrenia. Another example is antidepressant drugs such as Prozac which reduce the rate that neurotransmitters are reabsorbed by nerve endings if they are not collected by a dendrite. They are known as selective serotonin reuptake inhibitors, or SSRIs, because they inhibit the reabsorption of serotonin. They can also block the effect of an enzyme which breaks down excess neurotransmitters. Both of these methods increase the amount of serotonin that is available in the brain for neighbouring neurons.

<< CHAPTER 8

EVOLUTION OF BRAIN STUDIES

Early methods: Dissection

Early attempts to study the anatomy of the brain used post-mortem dissections. The brains of patients with cognitive defects were examined after death to see which areas of the brain showed damage or difference to a normally functioning brain. This gave us a good knowledge of the anatomy of the brain, but only a limited knowledge of how a living brain functioned.

1950s: Positron Emission Tomography (PET) Scans

PET scans involve injecting a small amount of a radioactive tracer into a patient (for example, radioactive glucose). The tracer collects in more active areas of the brain and then can be detected by a scanner. This allows us to measure the metabolic activity in different areas of the brain when a patient performs a specific task. Unfortunately, this method of analysis can cause damage to brain tissue.

1920s: Electroencephalography (EEGs)

An EEG involves placing electrodes on the scalp of a living patient and measuring the electrical activity in different areas of the brain. This allows us to study living, working brains without harming a patient, but only gives limited information and is not very good at pinpointing exact areas of activity.

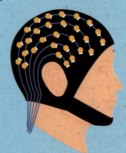

BIOLOGICAL THEORY >> 103

1980s: Magnetic Resonance Imaging (MRI)

An MRI is produced by placing the patient in a large magnetic field. This causes positively charged protons in the atoms of the brain to line up with the direction of the magnetic field. When the magnet is turned off, they return to their original position and release electromagnetic waves, which are detected by a scanner to produce an image. While this method also only shows us a snapshot of the brain, it has the advantage of not using any potentially damaging radiation, unlike PET and CAT scans.

1960s: Computerized Tomography (CAT or CT) Scans

During a CAT scan a patient is placed in a large rotating scanner that takes X-rays of the brain. A computer is then used to analyse the images and produce a detailed picture of the brain. This method allows us to see detailed images of the structure of the brain, but is only a snapshot and does not show us the brain as it is working.

1990s: Functional Magnetic Resonance Imaging (fMRI)

fMRI scans measure blood flow to different areas of the brain and therefore can show which specific areas of the brain are working in real time. The magnetic properties of blood cells change when they are carrying oxygen compared to when they are not. More active areas of the brain require more oxygen, and this difference is picked up by the fMRI scan. fMRIs have many applications, one particularly exciting example being communicating with patients who appear to be in a vegetative state.

Chapter 9

Social Psychology

Social Facilitation

Conformity

Obedience

SOCIAL PSYCHOLOGY >>

HUMANS ARE A SOCIAL SPECIES. We evolved to live in social groups that provided support in a variety of ways, through cooperation, protection, resourcing, and learning from one another. Now we rely on our interconnected societies to also provide us with the luxuries of our modern lives, with technology providing even greater and more varied methods of interaction and socialization.

Influential psychologist Gordon Allport described social psychology as 'an attempt to understand and explain how the thoughts, feelings and behaviour of individuals are influenced by the actual, imagined, or implied presence of others' (1985). Psychologists have studied how the presence of others affects aspects of our behaviour such as our judgement, decision making and motivation.

ASSUMPTIONS

A social approach to psychology assumes that other people influence our behaviour and thought processes. This can occur even when other people are not actually present. It also assumes that our relationships with others, and the nature of those relationships, influence our behaviour. For example, in this chapter we will investigate obedience and how the perceived authority of another person may influence how we interact with them and whether we follow instructions from them. We will also look at how the presence of others may cause us to conform to the opinion of a group even when we may believe the group is wrong.

SOCIAL FACILITATION THEORY

Much research in this area has originated in the USA, with the earliest generally regarded to have been conducted by Norman Triplett (1861–1934), which is also often credited with being the first research study conducted in the field of sport psychology. He developed a concept which later came to be known as 'social facilitation theory'. This theory proposes that

ESSENTIAL PSYCHOLOGISTS

Gordon Allport
Lived: 1897–1967
Origin: United States of America
Known for: Personality Psychology

people's effort on a task is influenced by the presence of others, whether they are actually there or it is simply implied that they are there.

Triplett's research in 1898 involved cyclists trying to beat a record in three different conditions; a race against time, paced race against time, and paced competition race.

- In the first condition, the rider was asked to try to lower an established record, either to reduce their own or another man's time.
- In the second condition, a rider was asked to do the same thing but with a pacemaker bike setting a pace for them.
- In the third condition the pacemaker was present again as in condition two, but there was the added challenge that the rider was expected to compete in a race against others.

What Triplett found was that riders in the third condition performed best with the quickest times.

Condition	Average time per mile
25 miles unpaced against time	2 minutes 29 seconds
25 miles paced	1 minute 55 seconds
25 miles paced competition	1 minute 50 seconds

This is now known as the 'coordination effect' and forms part of a larger area of research known as 'social facilitation'. This is the idea that people will perform better or put more effort into a task in the presence of others, whether that presence is real or simply perceived.

However, this effect is not universal and in some cases psychologists have found that working as part of a group actually results in an effect known as 'social loafing'. In this case, people put less effort into a task when they are working as part of a group than they would do if they completed the task as an individual. This has been linked to factors such as group size, where one contributor may perceive that they can 'hide in the crowd' and their lack of effort go unnoticed, or they may feel that they have less of a responsibility as a result of being part of the group.

SOCIAL PSYCHOLOGY >>

In a cycle race, the presence of other riders leads to quicker times.

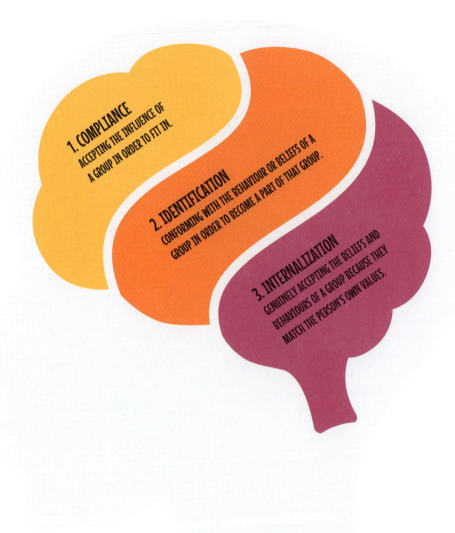

Social influence theory – the three factors linked to conformity.

KELMAN, ASCH AND CONFORMITY

Conformity is the act of changing a belief or behaviour in order to fit in with a group. Conformity may have benefits for a social species such as ours, enabling us to form cohesive groups who can work together for a common goal. However, conformity can also cause us to make incorrect judgements, be persuaded to behave in ways that do not match our own moral values, or even commit crime. Herbert Kelman (1927–2022), who first introduced his concept of social influence theory in 1958, suggested that conformity is linked to three factors – compliance, identification and internalization.

In 1951 Solomon Asch conducted a study which clearly demonstrated how the presence of a group could distort a person's judgement on a simple task, causing them to conform to the beliefs of the group.

In Asch's study participants were asked to compare a target line with three other lines and then state which of the three lines matched the target line. In order to avoid participants guessing the true aim of the study they were told this was a study investigating vision. Each participant was placed in a group of people known as 'confederates' who did know the true nature of the study and had been given pre-prepared answers for each question. The confederates began by giving the correct answers when shown the target and comparison lines, but after a few trials they began to choose incorrect answers. Asch was interested in whether or not the participants would give incorrect answers to the quite simple task in order to conform with the group. Asch found that 75 per cent of his participants gave an incorrect answer which matched that of the rest of the group at least once, and one participant conformed in 11 out of 13 trials.

ESSENTIAL PSYCHOLOGISTS

Solomon Asch
Lived: 1907–1996
Origin: Poland/United States of America
Known for: Personality Psychology

<< CHAPTER 9

Conformity.

KEY VOCABULARY

Co-action effect	Traits existing in an animal or person from birth, rather than those that can be learnt, essential to nature or character.
Social loafing	A single nerve cell transmitting and receiving electrochemical messages.
Conformity	Chemical messengers or molecules such as serotonin and dopamine that carry, enhance and balance signals between neurons and target cells throughout the body.
Authority figure	The cerebral cortex is the folded outer grey layer of the brain made up from tightly packed neurons. It is associated with various complex cognitive processes and higher-level functions including thought, memory, perception, attention, language, consciousness and advanced motor functions.
Despotic	A branch-like projection of a neuron that receives information from other neurons.
Extremism	The holding of extreme political views in opposition to conventional values, often associated with promoting extreme ideologies through hatred and violence.

Asch then repeated his study and varied certain factors to see how this would affect conformity rates. He changed the size of the group and found that with only one confederate the conformity rates dropped to 3 per cent. Conformity rates peaked at 32 per cent with three confederates, and with large groups conformity rates actually decreased. Conformity also dropped when one confederate disagreed with the group and gave the correct answer, and it also decreased if the participants were able to give their answers privately. However, if the task became more difficult and the correct answer more ambiguous then conformity increased.

Asch's research demonstrates the effect of group pressure on how we communicate our judgements. However, in this case the task had very low stakes and did not reflect the real life scenarios we may find ourselves in. From the participants' perspective there was no real or immediate risk to themselves or anyone else if they incorrectly matched the target line. One famous piece of research into a different type of social influence, the phenomenon of obedience to authority, certainly did use an element of risk to create a research situation with higher stakes.

ESSENTIAL PSYCHOLOGISTS

Stanley Milgram
Lived: 1933–1984
Origin: United States of America
Known for: Obedience

OBEDIENCE

Unlike conformity, which is the swaying of an individual's behaviour or belief to conform to that of a group, obedience is the ability of an authority figure (or a perceived authority figure) to influence the behaviour of one person or many people. Interest in this area of research increased in the wake of World War II when psychologists sought to answer the question of why seemingly 'normal' people could commit such cold and cruel acts as those that occurred during the Holocaust. Were they simply following orders? And if so, is this a universal human trait?

In 1963 Stanley Milgram (1933–84) conducted his famous study on obedience. His aim was to investigate whether a participant would submit a 'learner' to increasingly painful electric shocks when they gave incorrect answers to a series of questions simply because they had been asked to do so by a perceived authority figure. The learner was in fact a stooge who was pretending to receive electric shocks, but the participant would not find this out until after the study.

The participants were told that they were taking part in a study on learning and introduced to a stooge called Mr Wallace. The participant and Mr Wallace drew straws to randomly decide who would be the learner and who would be the teacher, but the draw was rigged so that Mr Wallace was always picked to be the learner. He then went into a different room and the participant was given their instructions. They were to ask Mr Wallace a series of questions through a microphone and if he gave an incorrect answer they were to use a machine to give Mr Wallace an electric shock. The participant was given a small 45 volt shock to show them that the equipment was real, and then they were to begin the procedures. Each time Mr Wallace gave an incorrect answer the participant was told to give him a shock that was 15 volts higher than the last.

To make the procedures appear real Mr Wallace would make certain pre-prepared noises that the participant could hear, such as grunts of pain when he received the alleged shocks. His responses to the shocks became more pronounced as they continued, with him making statements such as 'get me out of here'. He screamed loudly at 315 volts, and then made no noises from 330 volts onwards. The maximum voltage the participant could reach was 450 volts.

During the procedures the researcher, who represented the authority figure in this case, shared set statements to encourage the participant, for example saying 'please continue' or 'I am responsible for what happens'.

Milgram found that all of the participants that began the study continued up to 300 volts and 65 per cent continued all the way to 450 volts. He also noted that participants behaved in a way that implied they believed that the procedures in the study were real, with some sweating, trembling and showing other signs of stress such as digging their fingernails into their skin. Three participants became so overwhelmed that they had seizures, and one participant's seizure was so severe the experiment had to be stopped.

Milgram subsequently repeated his experiment and amended certain features. He found that by varying the location, clothing worn by the researcher, and the proximity of the learner to the participant he would find different levels of obedience.

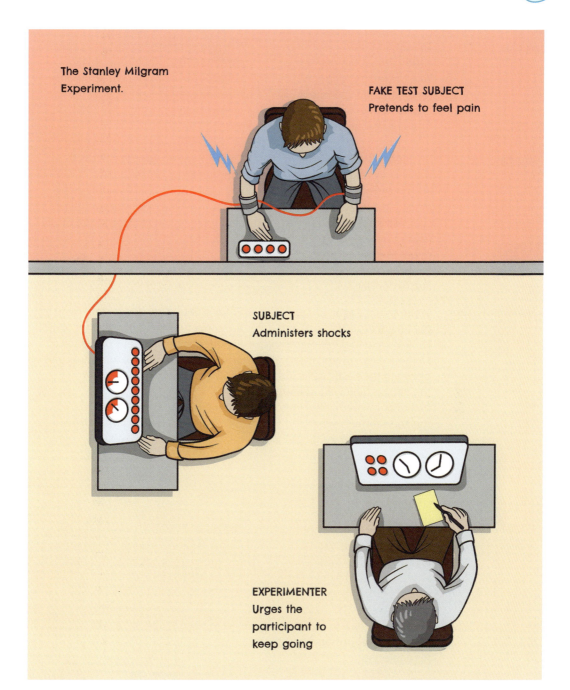

Location	The original study was conducted at the prestigious Yale University. Milgram repeated the experiment in a run-down building in Bridgeport, Connecticut.	The percentage of participants that continued the procedures to 450 volts fell from 65 per cent at the Yale laboratory to 47.5 per cent at the run-down building.
Clothing	In Milgram's original study the researcher (playing the authority figure) wore an official-looking white lab coat. Milgram repeated the procedures, replacing the researcher with a plain-clothed member of the public (who was also a stooge).	The percentage of participants that continued the procedures to 450 volts fell from 65 per cent when the researcher wore a lab coat, to 20 per cent with a plain-clothed member of the public.
Proximity of learner	In the original procedures the teacher (participant) and learner were in different rooms, so there was a physical barrier between the participant and the person they were seemingly harming. Milgram later altered this so that the teacher and learner were in the same room, and in another variation asked the teacher to physically place the learner's hand on to the shock plate.	When the teacher and learner were in the same room and the teacher could experience the learner's pain, face to face, obedience to 450 volts dropped to 40 per cent. When the teacher was asked to physically place the learner's hand on the shock plate, obedience to 450 volts fell to 30 per cent.
Proximity of authority figure	During the original conditions the researcher remained with the teacher and gave direct prompts to them. In one of Milgram's variations the researcher gave the initial instructions face to face, then left and gave further prompts via a telephone.	Obedience up to 450 volts fell from 65 per cent to 21 per cent when the researcher was not in the room with the participant.

SOCIAL PSYCHOLOGY >>

The events of World War II saw psychologists attempt to explain the reasons for the levels of conformity and obedience towards Hitler's politics in Nazi Germany. Brehm, Kassin and Fein (1999) went as far as to claim that no social psychologist had a greater impact than Hitler. Post-war it became imperative that the rise of despotic and extremist politics should be prevented to maintain a lasting peace. It was out of this landscape that the experiments by Milgram and other social psychologists were conceived. Although these were devised to determine why individuals would commit acts of violence towards others through blind obedience, the studies themselves raise moral and ethical concerns. The question around research ethics is one of the most contested issues in psychology. Approaches can be intrusive, transgress animal and human rights, and can be influenced by the views and ideologies of those conducting research, as in the case of the Milgram obedience studies. It is no wonder then, that there is considerable debate about the approaches to investigating psychological phenomena and mental processes that remain to this day.

Social psychology explores how we interact with others.

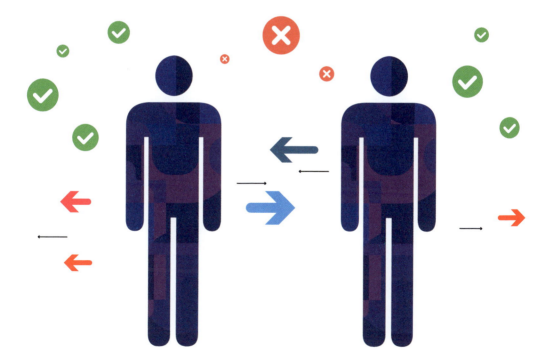

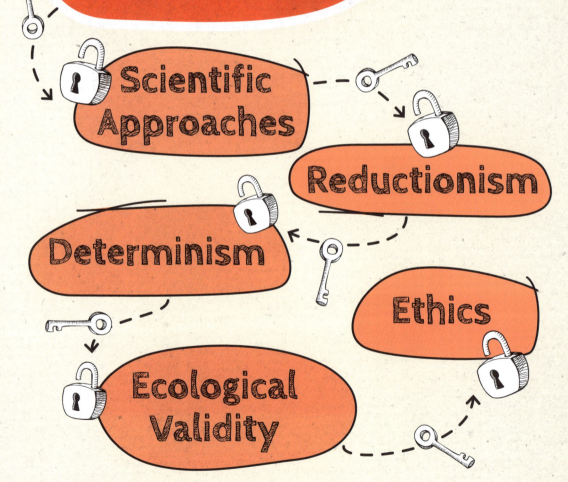

Chapter 10

DEBATES IN PSYCHOLOGY >> 117

WHAT INFLUENCES human behaviour is an incredibly complex question to explore. Studying human behaviour in a scientific and subjective way is not as straightforward as applying those same principles to chemical or physical processes, where extraneous factors can often be controlled and study conditions replicated.

While in chemistry every atom of an element will behave and react in a predictable and measurable way, and in physics the basic principles of forces remain constant, in psychology human behaviour can be unpredictable, variables uncontrollable, and findings difficult to replicate. There are also issues such as the social implications of psychological findings and how they influence our view of ourselves and others, as well as the ethics involved in actually conducting the research studies themselves. What is reasonable to expect human and animal subjects to endure in order for us to gain a greater understanding of behaviour?

There are a range of debates in psychology.

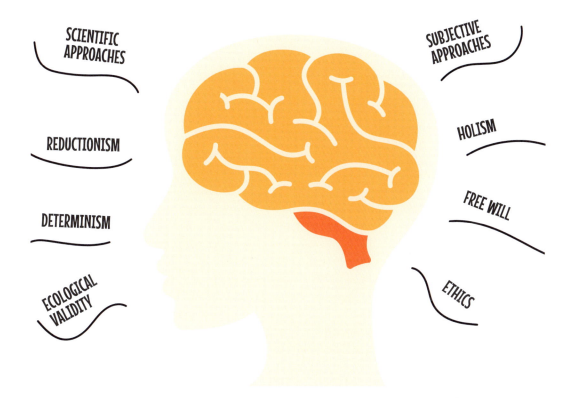

Psychologists have varied between taking scientific and subjective approaches to the subject.

SCIENTIFIC VERSUS SUBJECTIVE APPROACHES

Throughout this book we have discussed studies that use multiple different techniques to study the human mind and behaviour. From the more subjective case studies used by Freud to the pure cause and effect studies employed by the behavioural psychologists of the early 20th century, psychologists use many differing methods to make sense of our behaviour. Each method has its benefits and drawbacks, and all have contributed to our greater understanding of psychology.

Freud used case studies of his patients, himself, and in one famous case study a young boy called Hans to develop his theories. This methodology has the drawback of having a possible bias towards one particular group of people and therefore not be applicable to the wider population. Freud's patients would have been western European, quite specifically from Vienna, so can we be sure that his theories would be applicable to a person from an entirely different cultural background?

Another issue is that psychodynamic theories are often unfalsifiable. For an idea to stand up to scientific rigour it should be falsifiable, which means there should be a way to test the idea and attempt to prove it wrong. If many attempts to prove an idea wrong fail then that idea can be considered a well-established scientific theory. In the case of Freud and the psychodynamic approach, many theories are unfalsifiable by their very nature. If much of what is proposed occurs in the unconscious mind, how can it be studied?

DEBATES IN PSYCHOLOGY >>

What investigation could possibly be devised to test whether or not a child experiences the Oedipus complex?

There is now evidence from biological studies that could be used in support of some aspects of psychodynamic theory. For example, sleep studies have revealed that areas of the brain we may associate with Freud's concept of the ego, the areas associated with conscious thought, are dormant during sleep, whereas areas of the brain that could be associated with the id, the biological instincts, are more active. This would support Freud's suggestion that when we sleep the id is less constrained and our unconscious dreams and desires are able to penetrate our consciousness through dreams.

REDUCTIONISM VERSUS HOLISM

Approaches that use a more scientific methodology to study the mind and behaviour, such as the behaviourist approach, use strict controls to observe cause and effect. Studies such as those conducted by Pavlov (pages 53–55) and Watson and Raynor (pages 55–58) use carefully controlled conditions which could, theoretically, be replicated again and again by other researchers. They are able to control outside variables which may influence their results

Reductionism explains systems by looking at their most basic parts, while holism tries to examine the whole.

and therefore have a greater certainty that the response they are observing is most likely caused by the factor they controlled. A drawback of this methodology is that it can be accused of being reductionist.

Reductionism is the concept of analysing and explaining a complex system by reducing it down to its most basic and fundamental parts. In doing so, researchers risk over-simplifying explanations for complex behaviours and ignoring the fact that the behaviour may be influenced by many factors. For example, the biological approach suggests that depression may be caused by an imbalance of the neurotransmitter dopamine and can therefore be treated with drugs that affect the uptake of dopamine in the brain. It does not consider how influences from our environment, our emotions or our motivations may also contribute to feelings of depression.

In contrast to reductionism is holism. This approach attempts to consider 'the whole', so will consider multiple factors in order to explain behaviour. It would suggest that human experience is greater than the sum of its parts, and so we should consider as many factors as possible. Humanism is a branch of psychology which takes a holistic view of behaviour and goes so far as to reject the concept of large-scale scientific studies which aim to develop general theories that can be applied to all people. Research methods used to study psychology holistically could include qualitative research, such as case studies and interviews, which can be used to examine multiple possible explanations for a behaviour.

DETERMINISM AND FREE WILL

A further issue faced by psychology is the concept of determinism. Determinism is the implication that our actions and behaviours are caused by factors that are external to our will, that our behaviour is determined by our environment or our biology. For example, cognitive psychologists may claim that our fears are conditioned in us as children (see Watson and Raynor on (pages 55–58) whereas a biological psychologist may claim they are the result of our evolutionary past (pages 96–97).

A deterministic approach is useful in order to develop greater understanding of the causal factors of behaviour and therefore allow us to devise treatments for mental ill health. However, if the goal of a psychological theory is to find a cause for a behaviour that may be beyond our control, what role is there for free will? Without free will, can we be held accountable for our behaviour and actions? Studies such as Milgram's observation of the role of an authority figure (pages 111–114) would

DEBATES IN PSYCHOLOGY >>

certainly imply that humans are capable of committing acts that they would usually consider to be immoral when placed in an environment that diminishes the role of our free will.

A deterministic approach is often necessary when studying psychological ill health if we take the view that in order to treat an illness we should seek to find the possible causes of that illness. For example, psychodynamic theories which suggest that our behaviour is a result of our childhood experiences would certainly suggest a deterministic viewpoint. However, the concept that a person can alter their psychology through therapy suggests that we do have free will to take some control over our thoughts and behaviours.

Deterministic approaches to psychology

- Behaviourism – argues that behaviour is determined by our environment.
- Psychodynamic theory – behaviour is determined by our childhood experience.
- Cognitive theory – behaviour is determined by internal mental processes.
- Biological approach – behaviour is determined by the structure of our brain, hormones, neurotransmitters, genes, and our evolutionary past.

One key debate in psychology is whether we have the ability to determine our own actions.

ECOLOGICAL VALIDITY

Ecological validity in psychological research refers to the extent to which the procedures and therefore findings of a study can be compared to real life. If we wish to understand human behaviour in the real world we should aim to construct scenarios that truly test this, and the difficulty in doing so is a criticism of much research.

For example, Asch's study of conformity (pages 109–111) placed real participants in a scenario where they could choose to conform to a group and give an incorrect answer, or be true to their judgement and give a correct answer. The participants were real, they had not been informed that the rest of their group were actors, and it would seem therefore that their behaviours were genuine. However, we may not be able to generalize these findings to

real life conformity because the participants knew they were taking part in a psychological study in an artificial setting. Maybe they guessed the purpose of the study, or maybe they didn't feel that the stakes were very high. After all, they only had to state which line matched another. If the outcome of the task had greater significance they may not have conformed.

In any situation where a participant is aware of being watched and observed there is a risk that the behaviour they display is not ecologically valid. One solution to this problem is a type of research method known as 'covert observation', where people or groups of people are observed without their knowledge. However, this presents ethical issues such as a lack of consent from those taking part. How can you agree to be part of a research study if you have not even been asked?

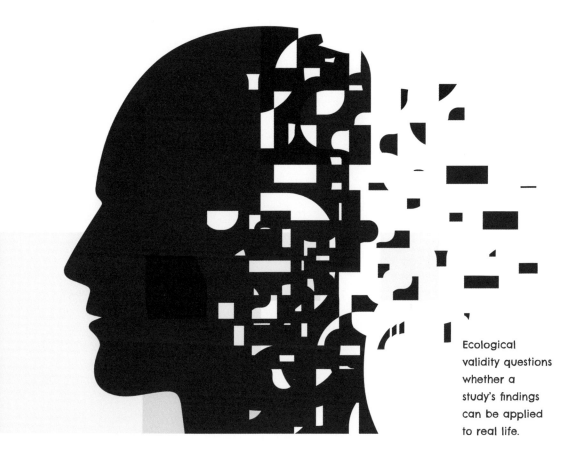

Ecological validity questions whether a study's findings can be applied to real life.

METHODOLOGIES USED TO STUDY PSYCHOLOGY	
Case studies	An in-depth study of one person, event or community. Often uses observations or interviews to gather data.
Observations	An investigation that measures behaviour in a particular environment. Can be covert (participants do not realize they are being watched) or overt (participants are aware they are being watched). Because observations can take place in real life settings they may be more likely to be ecologically valid.
Experiments	A study that includes an independent variable that is controlled by the experimenter, and a dependent variable that is measured by them in order to draw conclusions. There will usually be standardized procedures used and at least two different groups of participants.
Self-reports	Any measure that uses a participant's own report of their emotions or behaviours. Usually gathered using a questionnaire or interview.
Literature review	A piece of academic writing where a researcher reads previous research or publications on a topic and gives an overview of the research in that area. Their aim may be to describe and compare studies or to evaluate them. They will often suggest areas for future study.

ETHICS

Many of the historical studies we have discussed in this book raise ethical issues. The studies we have previously discussed by Milgram, and Watson and Raynor risked causing psychological harm to their participants. Studies using animals, such as Pavlov's research into classical conditioning and Skinner's operant conditioning research (pages 59–60), sometimes cause actual physical harm to their subjects. For example, in order to measure the salivation of the dogs in his studies Pavlov surgically attached glass collecting vials to the salivary glands of the dog. Even Seligman, the psychologist at the forefront of the positive psychology movement, worked on studies in which dogs were given electric shocks in order to investigate the phenomena of 'learned helplessness'.

Psychologists now have to abide by stricter ethical guidelines that are recommended by governing bodies such as the British Psychological

Society. Any study they plan to conduct has to be presented to an ethics committee, either run by their institution or by an external agency depending on how routine the research is. The committee will consider whether the study will cause psychological harm to the participants and if any potentially unethical practices which might be necessary for the study to work, such as deceiving the participants about the true nature of the study, are fully justified and proportionate.

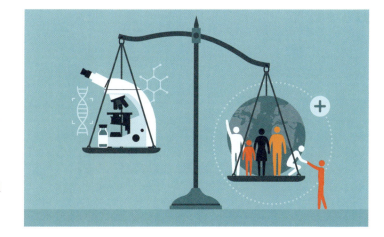

Much stricter ethical guidelines exist today for psychological research than in the past.

There are also certain procedures which should be followed when working with human participants. These include:

- Informed consent – Participants should be given enough information about the study that their consent, or agreement, to take part can be considered fully informed. In some cases the true intention of a study has to be kept secret from the participants otherwise it would affect the outcome of the study, but they should at least be given enough information to understand what they will experience.
- Confidentiality – As part of their briefing participants should be informed that their data will remain confidential. When recording their data, psychologists will often refer to their participants using numbers in order to maintain as much confidentiality as possible.
- The right to withdraw – Participants should be made aware that they have the right to remove themselves from the study at any time, even after it has started. They also have the right to have their data removed from the study at any reasonable time before it is published.
- Protection – Participants should be protected from both psychical and psychological harm. This includes embarrassment, fear or stress.
- Debrief – Once the study is over and there is no risk of affecting the outcome of the study, participants should be fully informed of what the true purpose of the study was and what benefits it may give to our understanding of psychology.

INDEX

adaptationist approach 96–7
Adler, Alfred 23
Allport, Gordon 105
analytical psychology 30–1
animal training 61
ape experiments 44–7
Aristotle 8
Asch, Solomon 109, 111, 122
Baddeley, Alan 65, 67
Bauhaus school 40
behaviourism
    assumptions of 51, 53
    and classical conditioning 53–8
    in everyday life 61
    key vocabulary in 52
    and operant conditioning 59–60
biological theory
    and adaptationist approach 96–7
    brain studies in 102–3
    and environment of evolutionary
adaptiveness (EEA) 96–7
    history of 95
    key vocabulary in 97
    and localization of function 96,
98–100
    and neurotransmission 100–1
    and psychodynamic theory 119
Bowlby, John 96
brain function 6–8, 96, 98–100
brain studies 102–3
Broca, Paul 100
Broca's area 100
Burckhardt, Gottlieb 95
classical conditioning 53–8
closure, principle of 38, 40
cognitive behavioural therapy (CBT) 73
cognitive development 70–3

cognitive psychology
    assumptions of 63–4
    and cognitive development 70–3
    in everyday life 73
    key vocabulary in 65
    and language and memory 67–9
    and short-term memory 65, 67
collective unconscious 31–2
common region, principle of 39
computerized tomography (CAT)
scans 103
conformity 108–11, 122–3
continuity, law of 36, 40
Descartes, René 8
determinism 120–1
Diener, Ed 92
dream analysis 33
dualism 8
ecological validity 122–3
ego 24, 28, 29, 30, 32, 33
electroencephalography (EEGs) 102
elementary sensations 18, 19
environment of evolutionary
adaptiveness (EEA) 96–7
ethics 124–5
Experimental Psychology (Titchener) 18
free will 120–1
Freud, Sigmund 23, 25–6, 27, 28, 29,
30, 32, 33, 95, 118–19
Friedrich, Max 14–15
functional magnetic resonance
imaging (fMRI)
functionalism 20
gambling 61
Gestalt theory
    and ape experiments 44–7
    assumptions of 35–9

and closure 38, 40
and common region 39
and continuity 36, 40
and design 40
in everyday life 40
and Gestalt therapy 47–9
key vocabulary in 42
and optical illusions 41, 43
and prägnanz 36
and proximity 38
and similarity 37
Gestalt therapy 47–9
good life 83, 86–7, 92
Griffiths, Mark D. 21
happiness 83, 86–7, 92
hierarchy of needs 75, 77–9
history of psychology 8–9
Hobbes, Thomas 8
holism 119–20
humanistic approach
    assumptions of 74
    and Carol Rogers 79–83
    good life in 83
    key vocabulary in 76
    and Maslow's hierarchy of needs
75, 77–9
    and person-centred therapy 79–80
    and self-concept 81–2
id 24, 28, 29, 30, 32, 33
Institute for Experimental Psychology
13–15
introspection 14–15, 16, 19, 20, 21
Jessen, Bruce 91
Jung, Carl 23, 26, 30–2
Kant, Immanuel 8–9
Kelman, Herbert 109
Klein, Melanie 23

Koffka, Kurt 35, 40, 45
Köhler, Wolfgang 35, 40, 41, 44–5
language and memory 67–9
learned helplessness 88–91
'Little Albert' study 55–8
localization of function 96, 98–100
Locke, John 8
Loftus, Elizabeth 67–8, 72
magnetic resonance imaging (MRI) 103
Maier, Steven 88, 90
manifest content 33
Maslow, Abraham 75, 77–9, 83
memory 64, 65, 67–9
Milgram, Stanley 111–14, 120, 124
Mitchell, James E. 91
Motivation and Personality (Maslow) 78
Müller, Johannes 12
multi-store model of memory 64
Myers, David 92
neurotransmission 100–1
obedience 111–15
operant conditioning 59–60
optical illusions 41, 43
Outline of Psychology, An (Titchener) 19
Palmer, John 67–8, 72
Pavlov, Ivan 53, 55, 88, 119, 124
Perls, Friedrich S. 47
Perls, Laura 47
person-centred therapy 79–80
phi phenomenon 41, 43
Piaget, Jean 70
positive psychology
    assumptions of 85–6
good life in 86–7, 92
key vocabulary in 86
and learned helplessness 88–91
and Martin Seligman 85, 86, 88–91

Positron Emission Tomography (PET)
scans 102
prägnanz 36
Principles of Physiological Psychology
(Wundt) 13, 15
proximity, principle of 38
psychic determinism 24
psychodynamic theory
    assumptions of 24–7
    and biological theory 119
    and Carl Jung 23, 26, 30–2
    and dream analysis 33
    in everyday life 33
    key vocabulary in 25
    and Sigmund Freud 23, 25–6, 27,
28, 29, 30, 32, 33
        subjective approaches in 118–19
        and tripartite mind 24, 28–30
Psychology of the Unconscious (Jung) 30
psychosexual stages 25–7
Raynor, Rosalie 55–8, 119, 120, 124
reductionism 119–20
Rogers, Carl 79–83, 86
schemas 64, 70
scientific approaches 118–19
self-concept 81–2
Seligman, Martin 85, 86, 88–91, 124
short-term memory 65, 67
similarity, law of 37
Skinner, B. F. 59, 61
social facilitation theory 105–7
social groups 7–8
social psychology
    assumptions of 105
    conformity in 108–11
    obedience in 111–15
    and social facilitation theory 105–7

sound cage experiment 18
structuralism 16–21
structuralist theory
    assumptions of 11–12
    in everyday life 21
    and functionalism 20
    and Institute for Experimental
Psychology 13–15
    and introspection 14–15, 16, 19,
20, 21
        key vocabulary in 14
        and structuralism 16–21
        and Wilhelm Wundt 12–15
subjective approaches 118–19
superego 24, 28, 29–30, 32, 33
Titchener, Edward 11, 12, 15–16, 18,
19–20
tripartite mind 24, 28–30
Triplett, Norman 105–6
von Helmholtz, Hermann 12, 13
Washburn, Margaret Floy 16
Watson, John B. 51, 53, 55–8, 119,
120, 124
Wernicke, Carl 100
Wernicke's area 100
Wertheimer, Max 35, 40, 41, 45
Wundt, Wilhelm 11, 12–15, 16

PICTURE CREDITS

t = top, b = bottom

Alamy: 38b, 96, 113

Getty Images: 35, 51, 70, 75, 80, 85, 109, 111

thenounproject.com: 58

Science Photo Library: 46

Shutterstock: 7, 8, 9, 11 (x3), 15, 16, 17, 18, 21, 23, 24, 26, 28, 30, 31, 33, 36 (x2), 37, 39 (x2), 40, 42, 47, 48, 54, 60, 61, 63, 66, 69, 72, 73, 77, 79, 87, 93, 95, 98, 99, 101, 102, 103, 105, 107, 108, 110, 115, 117, 118, 119, 121, 123, 125

Topfoto: 45

Wikimedia Commons: 12, 13, 19, 38t, 53, 59, 90